J.S. BRACEWELL
Lawyer

By his sons, Searcy and Fentress Bracewell

Dedicated to Lola Blount Bracewell,
Our Mother

Because she was always at his side,
and because he would have wanted it so dedicated.

Searcy and Fentress Bracewell

Contents

Acknowledgements

J. S. BRACEWELL, LAWYER is a project that has taken many years to put together. The book is a celebration of the life and accomplishments of our father, J. S. Bracewell, and is comprised mainly of his writings and recollections. We wish to acknowledge a number of people, without whose support and participation this project could not have been accomplished. Several people from Bracewell & Patterson, L.L.P. graciously contributed to this effort. Carlton Wilde and William Key Wilde, two of our partners, shared their remembrances of our father. Alice Fosson, librarian, provided her extensive research skills and library support to the project. Will Luedke, partner, and Ryan Holcomb, associate, read the manuscript and offered helpful suggestions.

In addition, several people from outside the firm assisted with this project. Waggoner Carr, former Texas Attorney General, graciously provided his recollections of our father, Dr. Noel M. Taylor, former President of The Broadway Plan and Rev. Harold E. Dye, pastor of the Baptist Temple in San Jose, California, shared their reminiscences and information about our father and The Broadway Plan. Also, William H. Kellar, Ph.D., Director of the Scholars' Community and Visiting Assistant Professor of History at the University of Houston, helped with the publishing process and book design.

Finally, we want to express our gratitude to Wanda Van Hook, our secretary at Bracewell & Patterson, L.L.P. "Miss Wanda" typed and edited many versions of the manuscript, collected photographs and documents, supervised the book design and, through it all, maintained an unflagging belief in this project.

Searcy and Fentress Bracewell

Foreword

On December 28, 1917, our father, J. S. Bracewell, then 25 years of age, wrote a letter to Judge J. A. Elkins seeking a job with the newly-formed firm of Vinson & Elkins. Among other things, Dad said:

"...The best estimate I could make of my practice in the summer was $60.00 per month—cash. Things look better now and I think I can safely count on carrying anywhere from $75.00 to $100.00 to your firm from the beginning."

He did not get the job, but he pursued another course which eventually brought him success and esteem in the legal profession.

From his early years, he had ambitions of becoming a lawyer. However, the dire financial circumstances of this tenant-farming family of seven children dictated that he forego his ambition to study law until he could accumulate enough funds to enroll in a one-year law course at Cumberland University in Lebanon, Tennessee. First, he managed to attend Sam Houston State Teachers' College in Huntsville, Texas—long enough to qualify as a school teacher in the rural school at Roans Prairie—a small town near Bedias—where he earned the money to make the trip to Tennessee. One of his pupils in the one-room school at Roans Prairie was Lola Blount, whom he married on December 24, 1916.

Born to humble, devoutly religious tenant farmers in a small Texas town between Bryan and Huntsville on June 9, 1892, he had to fight for an education and then struggle to establish himself in the practice of law. But thanks to his keen mind, ringing rhetoric, bulldog determination and to the unfailing and cheerful support of our mother, he went on to found one of the largest and most successful law firms in Texas— Bracewell & Patterson, L.L.P. He also developed The Broadway Plan, a method for funding church building through the sale of revenue bonds. Thanks to this program, over 3,000 congregations throughout the United States and Canada were able to build and expand into modern, comfortable structures.

Along the way, Dad campaigned for some of Texas' most colorful political candidates and backed causes that set the direction for Houston and the state. He even sought office himself, unsuccessfully running for Harris County District Attorney in 1922—a time when that office and much of local politics were controlled by the Ku Klux Klan. Toward the end of his life, he spent two years as head of Texas Attorney General Waggoner Carr's Natural Resources Division during a period when growing environmental awareness and the state's booming economy made that task especially challenging. He also helped found California Baptist College and lectured there regularly on the Bill of Rights.

Dad's days at Cumberland Law School were apparently very enjoyable, because he often reflected on them. He took an active part in debating, extemporaneous speaking, and the literary societies at the school, considering this most important to his legal career and rarely missing an opportunity to speak on matters of current interest. Before the days of radio and television, public gatherings and speeches were an important part of every community.

In June 1915, after completing his one-year law course, he returned to Texas by way of Texarkana, where he stopped to take the bar examination. In those days, each court of civil appeals was authorized to give qualified applicants an examination for admission to the Texas bar. Not only was this a convenient stop for young J. S. Bracewell, but the Texarkana court was generally regarded to be the most lenient for the bar examination and, consequently, a favorite test site of aspiring young lawyers-to-be.

After returning to Texas, Dad moved to the town of Harrisburg (now in Houston's east side), where he taught school and practiced law from a one-room office behind the Harrisburg Drug Store.

Harrisburg deserves special mention because it was an important factor in Dad's career. Located some six miles from the center of downtown Houston where Brays Bayou runs into Buffalo Bayou, the town had much historical significance. It was older than Houston and was once the capital of Texas before it was burned by Santa Ana and his Mexican forces as they came through in pursuit of General Sam Houston a few days before their encounter at San Jacinto.

When Dad settled in Harrisburg, he plunged into the civic affairs of this small community by teaching school, practicing law, and being active in church work and political affairs. There was a small wooden courthouse where the justice of the peace and the constable of that precinct had their office, courtroom, and jail. As youngsters, we often went to court with our father. The courtroom was upstairs. Since there was no air conditioning in those days, the windows of the courtroom were kept open and the people would gather around outside the building to hear the lawyers argue to the jury. Dad had a tremendous voice—when he argued a case, you could hear him all over town. Harrisburg had another lawyer or two, but J. S. Bracewell was by far the most active.

In 1922, at a time when the Ku Klux Klan was the principal political issue, Dad ran for district attorney as an anti-Klan candidate. In the early 20s, the candidates for office endorsed by the Klan were generally the winners. Dad was defeated by the Klan-endorsed candidate, but his tireless campaigning throughout the county brought him recognition. This name identification—coupled with his reputation as a two-fisted trial lawyer representing the underdog clients of his day—established him as one of the leading attorneys in Houston.

During the 1920s and 1930s, Dad shared offices with several lawyer friends, including A. E. Dawes, H. H. Cooper, Harry Gerlach, Charles B. Spiner, Quinton Wright, Fred Parks, Jess Pardue and Bert Tunks. He was politically active throughout his life, although he never held elective office. The lure of public service found him working for a time as an assistant district attorney under John H. Crooker, who later became one of the founders of the law firm of Fulbright & Jaworski.

In almost every major political race in the 1920s and 1930s, Dad took an active role. It was not his nature to be passive about anything. If a matter interested him, he jumped in with both feet. One of our earliest recollections of Dad's political activities was accompanying him to political rallies, which were very popular before the days of television and when radio was in its infancy. These were gatherings where the candidates or their representatives were invited to speak. Rallies were held all over the county—sometimes several on the same night—so it was necessary for a candidate to have support from volunteer speakers. Dad enjoyed going to rallies and speaking for candidates he was supporting. He actively backed Miriam A. Ferguson in her races for governor. He was most active in the race of R. H. Spencer against incumbent Judge Ward for county judge. He took an active role in Walter Montieth's successful race against Oscar Holcombe for Mayor of Houston. And in 1940, Dad was Harris County campaign manager for Wendell Wilkie in his campaign against Franklin D. Roosevelt for the presidency, believing that no person should serve as President for more than two terms. Dad was appointed chairman of the Houston Port Authority on October 1, 1954, where he served until May 28, 1956.

No lawyer in Houston was more involved in public issues than J. S. Bracewell during the 25-year period from 1920 to 1945. These were interesting, but extremely difficult years. In the early 20s, things were settling down following World War I. In the late 20s and early 30s, issues of human rights were just beginning to surface. Dad loved to challenge the establishment on such matters as fair trials for minorities and became very well known as a fighting and aggressive lawyer. His practice was oriented to the problems of those years. He was anxious to tackle difficult cases—usually the kind we would now call consumer oriented. His political beliefs, however, were conservative and pro-business. He believed in free enterprise. Although Dad believed strongly in the system, he loved to invoke the technical provisions of the law to the benefit of the downtrodden client.

Dad's way with a jury was amazing—a combination of basic honesty (which literally exuded from his countenance and personal decorum), his uncanny way of relating to the average man (who was serving on the jury), and his *great* skill at jury argument. We cannot over-emphasize the latter. Dad strongly believed that after all the evidence had been presented and the judge had given his charge, the jury *expected an oration*. He often said that the jurors felt disappointed if they didn't get to hear an oration when it came time to argue the case. He was loud, he pounded on the table, he paced to and fro, he pointed his finger at his adversary, and he shouted. He radiated righteous indignation at the injustice suffered by his client, but he was unfailingly courteous and kind. The jury nearly always decided the case in his favor, even though the law may not have been on his side. Crowds would gather in the courtroom when word spread through the courthouse that J. S. Bracewell was about to make a jury argument.

He was respected and admired by his friends among the lawyers in Houston and was elected President of the Houston Bar Association in 1937.

During the years following World War II, Dad devoted more and more of his time to The Broadway Plan and, together with our mother, traveled extensively throughout the country visiting churches which had made inquires about the program. Dad and Mother gave their home in Harrisburg to the Broadway Baptist Church for use as a school and moved to Roans Prairie, living in our mother's old homestead—known as "The Farm." They did much traveling between 1945 and 1965, but between trips enjoyed their lives in Grimes County where their roots were.

In 1963, however, the Texas Attorney General, Honorable Waggoner Carr, prevailed on Dad to take on duties as an Assistant Attorney General. He accepted this challenge, and the couple commuted back and forth to the state capitol from Roans Prairie for a couple of years before his death on November 30, 1965. (Fortuitously, in the summer of that year, we hosted a reception at The Houston Club to which all members of the Houston Bar were invited to mark Dad's 50 years as a practitioner at the Texas bar.) Our mother continued to live at "The Farm" until her death on August 4, 1985.

J. S. Bracewell was a man of his time, of his place, and of his profession. His personal history offers a window into day-to-day life in East Texas at the first part of the 20th century and into Houston's transformation from a provincial town into a major city. He was a member of a now all but extinct breed—a country lawyer in the city. Along with his speeches, lectures, and jury trial arguments, the events of Dad's life also reflect the transition of the legal profession from the days of the silver tongued and largely independent, self-taught generalist to the present era of rigorous academic training and narrow specialization.

When he was in his late 60s and early 70s, Dad began writing down some of his recollections. His memory for detail—from the pleading look in the eyes of a helpless defendant or the color of the dress our mother wore on the evening he proposed—is uncanny. He had no hobby other than his practice of law and the devotion to his church. He was a prolific writer and most of this book contains his actual writings on various subjects—with little editing.

Our father was a lawyer—through and through. He had no business interests on the side. He did not play golf. He did not play tennis. He was not interested in hunting. He did not fish.

Dad died when he was only 73, but he lived a very productive life—making every day count in some way. He personified the person whom the poet described:

> *Count that day lost whose low descending sun,*
> *Views from thy hand no worthy action done.*

We hope this book will give members of our family, our friends, and the law firm a sense of J. S. Bracewell—both the lawyer and the man. We also hope it will be of interest to students of legal thought, of state and local history, and of everyday life in early 20th century Texas.

Searcy Bracewell and Fentress Bracewell

Chapter 1

Growing Up in East Texas: J. S. Bracewell's Early Years

The Boy from Sand Hill

As I attained success and recognition as a lawyer, I became known in Houston and beyond as "J. S." (Joseph Searcy), but as a child growing up in rural East Texas, I was called Searcy. I was born June 9, 1892, in the Sand Hill community about 4 miles from the small town of Bedias, in Grimes County. My parents—tenant farmers Buddy and Mollie Shanks Bracewell—named me after their favorite preacher, Reverend Searcy. Old Parson Searcy from Willowhole Prairie was a frequent substitute for the regular pastor of Mount Pleasant Baptist Church, which the Bracewells attended. The people liked to hear him preach better than they did their own elder, except for a peculiarity which sometimes negated the homiletic import of his sermon. Once he got on shouting ground, the full immersionist became a sprinkler, spitting all over his white, stiff-bosomed shirt! When Parson Searcy held forth in the pulpit, the first row back of the mourners' bench was empty.

Parson Farrer, the regular pastor and a one-legged Civil War veteran, did not spit all over the pulpit, but he had a way of emphasizing his high points with a stomp of his pegged leg. This was the signal for a frenzied outburst of loud "Amens." So, while Parson Searcy was a little hard on the eyes and the aesthetic sensibilities, Parson Farrer was even harder on the ears. Both were upright, God-fearing men with love in their hearts and Bible wisdom in their words.

Sand Hill, in the early 1890s, was an interesting kind of place. There were no frills. Snuff-bottle lamps were the nearest thing to R.E.A. illumination. No railroad came within miles.

The center of religious, social, and civic life was Mount Pleasant Baptist Church. Buddy and Mollie Bracewell were charter members. Its nursery was a pallet in front of the preaching rostrum. Mothers put their babies there where they could be watched during the services. This was my first "pew" at church. "And," I recollected later in life, "it was the most comfortable I have ever had. We were actually expected to sleep in it. Now I have to sit straight up and do it surreptitiously!"

Mount Pleasant was what was known as a "half-time" church. That is to say, it had preaching twice a month. Its pastor had two other "quarter-time" churches, days apart in distance. In order to get the most out of an experience so precious in their lives, the congregation at Mount Pleasant had Saturday night services and preaching three times on Sunday. Sermons were sometimes two hours long. One preacher gave four two-hour sermons a weekend with four titles: "First Discourse on Hell," "Second Discourse on Hell," "Third Discourse on Hell," and "Fourth Discourse on Hell." Nobody thought of leaving. By the time he was finished, everyone school age and up knew the exact differences among Sheol, Tarturus, Hades, and Gehanna. The sermons reeked of brimstone, but the congregants liked them. It was all part of the Bible and, therefore, the Word of God. After all, there were also sermons on Heaven—tender, moving interpretations of that land where God would wipe away all tears from their eyes and there would be no more death, nor sorrow, nor crying, nor pain. "And," shouted Parson Farrar, "no peg legs would ever walk on the streets paved with gold!"

Of equal importance in the community was the school. Sand Hill boasted the best school in a ten-mile radius. It was a structure on the high sand hill, which was blanketed with grass burrs and hickory nuts. The school house was one room with a door in the middle on either side, making it specially adapted to a long-line spelling bee. Drinking water was fetched from a well about 200 yards away, and the boys would vie with each other to be one of the two to bear it in a bucket suspended on a pole resting on the shoulders.

Plumbing was unknown. The road extending down the hill through the wooded area to the west was considered "girl territory," and that on the south, in another patch of screening woods, was "boy territory." It was presumed that dire consequences would attend the breaking of this rule of eminent domain, though no one ever tested it.

At Sand Hill School, I broke into the academic world in 1897. I was five years old. I was plump, bow legged, red haired, freckle faced, and barefoot. Because of my bare feet, I approached the school house on my first day at school with a series of strident yells. My feet were shod with grass burrs. Finally, I could not go on—I could not go back—and I could not even sit down. It was then that my cousin Anna, who was blessed with a pair of brand-new, high-button shoes, rescued me. She bear-hugged me across the grass patch and, amid yelps of protest, pulled the torturing grass burrs from my tender feet. Then she ushered me into the presence of Miss Ophelia Grissett, the new school marm.

Miss Ophelia's three-year tenure exercised a remarkable influence on the community. She organized a literary and debating society which met once every month and considered such erudite questions as "Which is more pleasure, pursuit or possession?" and "Resolved, that Abraham Lincoln was a friend of the South." Her agenda even included drama and poetry.

Into all this, I entered most enthusiastically. It was at about this time I made my first speech—the first of hundreds during my lifetime. My red hair and freckled face made a fitting complement to my checkered coat, red necktie and button shoes. I brought the house down by stepping out boldly and proclaiming:

A Boston master said one day,
'Tell me, boys, I pray,
Why Washington's birthday should shine
in today's history
More than mine.'

There was such stillness in the hall
You could have heard a feather fall,
When exclaimed a boy not three feet tall,
'He never told a lie.'

My elocutionary performance led to frequent appearances on the programs of the Sand Hill Literary Society.

Of course, Sand Hill had other cultural pursuits. *The Galveston Dallas Semi-Weekly Farm News* kept the community fairly well-informed on current events, both at home and abroad. What mattered if it was two or three weeks old? It was still news when it got there. One day the paper reported that some fellow by the name of Tom Edison had invented a talking machine. Miss Ophelia got pretty excited about that. She was determined to see and hear the marvelous contraption herself, and—always mindful of community interests—was also determined that the rest of the citizens would see and hear one, too.

Miss Ophelia threw the community into a tizzy by suddenly announcing that the school building had been reserved by the blind fiddler, Manny Plaster, for a musical concert with his daughters. The ensemble was to include a banjo, a guitar, a drum, and a tambourine. And, wonder of wonders, he was to have at the musical festival the incredible talking machine. Notwithstanding the ten-cent admission charge, the crowds poured in, mostly coming to town on foot. They came early, realizing that the school house would be filled to standing room only.

But Uncle Manny did not reveal the hook in the bait. After a few "breakdowns" by the five-piece band, there was a sudden hush. Miss Ophelia had stepped into the center of the stage. With a dramatic flourish she whipped a white cloth from a table where, reposed in all its splendor, a brass-trimmed oaken box—out of the top of which came a huge metal horn shaped like a gigantic morning glory.

Very impressively the teacher cranked the machine and moved a lever. Out of the horn roared the pulse-quickening strains of "Turkey in the Straw." Next, feet were set tapping at the stirring cadence of "Arkansas Traveler." There was an excited murmur of voices.

It was then that Uncle Manny dynamited the works. He took the stage and announced that a silk handkerchief would be awarded to the prettiest girl present. And (here was the hook), votes would be cast at ten cents per. The crowd was in a mellow mood. Nominations began echoing in the hall. For a long time there had been spirited arguments in the community as to who was the prettier, my Aunt Ida Bracewell or Rose Midkiff. Now was the time to settle the arguments. What did it matter if the decision was more financial than it was pulchritudinous?

The talking machine was forgotten. The contest was long, loud, and exciting. With every vote cast, the total was announced. Since every swain present was honor bound to vote for his own girl, Uncle Manny had a sure thing going for him. In fact, he pocketed a total of $17 over and above the admission fees.

Besides the school and the church, there was another focal point for culture in the Sand Hill settlement. That was the home of my Uncle Barto Bracewell. Barto was a sort of human pendulum. More than any other man, he made the area tick. Probably, it was because of his varied interests. He was a prosperous farmer, yet his abundant energy allowed him to run a blacksmith shop, serve as dentist, and act as a pill roller and also as a coffin builder. Barto installed an organ in his home and invited talented singers. As they performed, he would lean back in his chair and a dreamy look would come over his leather face while his soul would be transported to the very fringes of heaven.

Such, as the century turned, was my world. It was a land of wagons, buggies, cotton gins, coffee mills, corn shellers, Brogan shoes (patent leather on Sunday), stiff-bosomed shirts and celluloid collars, rats (these were worn in the hair), bustles (these were worn on the rear), fascinators, high-top shoes and floor-sweeping dresses; of Calomal, quinine water, Smith's Chill Tonic, asafoetida (which warded off all manner of diseases—and friends and enemies too!), and castor oil (which cured everything which asafoetida could not prevent).

Now, only dreams linger on in Sand Hill. Old Mount Pleasant

Church has long since been torn down. Only the cemetery remains. Under the fading tombstones of the little cemetery sleep those whose influence was flung to the far corners of the earth: the Bracewells, Midkiffs, Shanks, Disonghs, Dooleys, Longs, Tucks, Morgans, Stones, Akins, Stufts, Boneys, Halls, Plasters, and others. They are in God's hands.

◆◆◆

Going to Court with My Father

I WAS BARELY out of grade school when I announced that I was going to become a lawyer. I might as well have stated that I was going to become a horse thief! It was the consensus of Sand Hill that an honest man could not be a lawyer.

When I was 13, my father and I went to court. One day, the sheriff rode up to the lfittle farmhouse and asked if my father, Buddy—as he was known by family and friends—was at home. Recognizing him as being a high officer of the law, my mother, Mollie, and the children were consternated. Why would the law be looking for a man who had led such a peaceful and inoffensive life? Mollie sent me scurrying to the adjoining field where my daddy and his older brothers, Emmett and Ernest, were plowing the stumpy ground.

Breathlessly assembled, the family stood mute as the sheriff read the summons to appear before the 12th District Court of Grimes County in Anderson, Texas—two weeks hence—to serve as a juror in the case of *State vs. Craft*. I immediately asked to go to Anderson with my father.

Since there were no trains from Bedias to Anderson (the county seat of Grimes County)—a distance of about 18 miles—Buddy decided to take the wagon and sleep in the wagon yard. That would save the hotel expense and bring the cost of the trip in line with the five cents per mile and dollar per day paid for jury service.

Nowadays, Anderson is hailed as one of the historic spots of Texas. Here sleeps Kenneth Anderson, third vice-president of the Republic of Texas. Anderson was also home to Alamo hero, Tapley Holland, and to the Texas Baptist Convention, which was organized at a local Baptist Church just beyond the Fanthorpe Stage Coach Inn, where General Sam Houston sometimes bunked. And history was still in the making. Few bar associations in the United States could boast a membership to compare with that of the 12th Texas District of that day. There were: Col. W. W. Meachum, probably one of the greatest lawyers Texas has produced; E. A. Berry, later on the Court of Criminal Appeals; Ben H. Powell, later on the Supreme Court; Capt. J. C. Hutcheson, later a congressman; Gordon and Hood Boone; Col. T. A. Buffington and T. A. Buffington, Jr.; Senator W. L. Dean; H. L. Lewis; M. E. Gates, Ben and Andy Campbell; J. G. McDonald; J. A. Elkins; W. L. Hill; Carl T. Harper; Jim Brownlee; and District Attorney Elmer Pope. All distinguished themselves as lawyers, judges, and legislators.

The bailiff was a striking figure—stocky, notch eared, and red faced, with thick lips and granulated eyelids. At 9 a.m. he went to the street-side window on the second floor and intoned in a booming voice: "Oh, yea! Oh, yea! The Honorable District Court of Grimes County, 12th District of the State of Texas, is now opened pursuant to adjournment. God save the Constitution of the United States and this Honorable Court!"

Lawyers, prospective jurors, litigants, witnesses, and spectators began to flood out of the hotels, saloons, stores, and wagons to be on hand when the gavel fell calling the docket. The courtroom was crowded and the veniremen were seated on the first rows. I was permitted to sit with my father and, consequently, had a ringside seat. As Judge Smither called the cases, the lawyers rose in great solemnity and answered "ready" or "not ready."

Finally, the case of *State vs. Craft* was called, and Col. Meachum announced that he was not ready for the defense. District Attorney Pope, answering for the State, insisted the case go to trial. Fortunately for me—and unfortunately for my father—the case was set for Friday. That gave me a chance to hear several other cases argued by different lawyers, but the dollar per day and mileage had to be sliced very thin to cover the expenses. I soon caught the general drift of qualifying the jurors, examining the witnesses, and finally, and most important in my mind, making the argument to the jury.

It was all very exciting. What I couldn't understand was how the lawyers could engage in bitter combat during the day, then at night eat together, drink together, and play dominoes and cards, apparently with great affection toward one another. A few hours earlier, one might have scathingly castigated the defendant as a hog thief and pulled for him to be sent to the penitentiary as the one way to stop hog stealing. The other might have argued for freedom on the basis of reasonable doubt or the plight of the accused's wife and children. The skillful defense lawyers seemed able to make black look white. They presented the tendency to commit wrongs as being born of weaknesses that almost amounted to virtues.

At last, the case of *State vs. Craft* came up. The jury list was called, but Buddy Bracewell's name wasn't on it. Being a timid man, he waited until court recessed to tell the judge he had been summoned and was entitled to his mileage and per diem. The judge said that when he failed to call the omission to his attention at the conclusion of the calling of the list, he had waived his right to payment. With the day already shot, my father and I stayed and listened to the case.

Craft had been charged with criminal assault on a child. Despite ample proof and aggravating circumstances, thanks to an eloquent plea by Col. Meachum, he got off with a relatively light sentence—two years in prison. Buddy Bracewell was stunned at the sentence. On our way home, he decided he had to express his outrage.

"The good Lord never intended that a guilty man go free," he announced with conviction.

"Hell, no, he didn't!" The words came from someone among the loungers on the porch of the Bedias store where we had stopped to pick up a sack of flour. Feeling against Jim Craft had been running pretty high all over Grimes County. Nowhere was it stronger than among these sturdy grassroots people who knew nothing and cared less of jurisprudential acrobatics. All they knew was Jim Craft was a skunk, and he ought to have been treated like one.

"Something else," said Buddy Bracewell. "The no-good lawyer who helps a guilty man go free is a tool of the devil and God is going to bring him to judgment, make no mistake!"

I listened in disbelief as his neighbors—even Elder Conway, a minister of the gospel—discussed shooting and lynching the man they thought the court had treated too leniently.

"See, what did I tell you?" Buddy Bracewell said on the four-mile ride from Bedias on to the farm. "An honest man just can't be a lawyer. Now you see that everybody else is of the same idea. I want you to give up your silly notion of going into such a dishonorable profession. I wish that you would be a farmer like me. I wish you would just join up with the good Lord as a partner to make the old black earth bring forth food for the people He put on it. Your mother wants you to be a preacher. So do I if you get the Call. If you hanker for something else, there's teaching school or keeping store. Then people would look up to you. But a lawyer!"

My usually-merry eyes were brooding. I was thinking of a saintly preacher and a shotgun, of a respected store manager and the words flung back from a slamming screen door: "Looks like if we want justice, we'll just have to take the matter in our own hands."

I was also thinking of a man sitting in a prisoner's dock— a black man with the dull, lusterless eyes of a subnormal. I was again hearing the skillful pleading of the man's counsel. I was hearing the vituperations of the district attorney, who seemed bent on being an avenging angel.

What would be the result if men were allowed to vent their individual and collective spleen against all those who broke their codes? What if a man thought guilty had no one to defend him? What if every man were prejudged without regard to ascertainable facts?

What if a guilty man did get off lightly now and then because of the skill of his attorney, compared to even one innocent man being condemned on circumstantial evidence? Did not God Himself want justice for all?

◆◆◆

Bedias

SAND HILL NEVER had to fight for land nor broaden its tax base by sly encroachment on nearby populated areas, but it had its part in the battle for survival. Four miles away was Bedias, and its residents had a way of getting in the hair of Sand Hill. Bedias had every intention of becoming a full-scale city. At first this intention was held by two or three merchants, but gradually the city-building fever swept the entire community.

Among those who settled in the Bedias area between 1821 and 1836 were I. Sims, John C. Corner, Abram Zuber, Isaac and Henry Midkiff, Thomas Plaster, Allen C. Jones, Keaton Jones, Samuel Bowman, James Pankey, James Moore and Daniel McMahan. I. Sims and John Corner arrived in the early 1820s, selected their homesites, staked out their claims, built their shanties and then made application to the Mexican government for land grants.

Still standing on the south side of North Bedias Creek after a century and a half, is the one and one-half story home of Allen C. Jones, a tough-sinewed cotton farmer. He felled cedar trees, set up the platform for a whip-saw, and laboriously cut the logs into slabs which he fitted together so carefully at the corners that they required no nails. Jones applied to the Mexican government for a land grant in 1834, but did not receive it until four years later—from the new Republic of Texas.

Gradually, around a few families, a town took shape. It was called Bedias, named after the Bidai Indians. *Bidai*, the Caddo word for brushwood, referred to the Big Thicket near the lower Trinity River—along which the Indians lived. The Bidai had their largest settlement in the northern part of Grimes County in the region of Black Lake Slough. There they had established their villages of bearskin huts. They hunted the region between the Colorado and Brazos Rivers, selling their furs at Nacogdoches. The Indian men did some farming, raising maize and later cotton, while their squaws wove baskets of intricate and beautiful design.

By the time I was ready for the second phase of my education, Bedias was a thriving village. It boasted two churches, Methodist and Baptist. Thus, pseudo-Baptists and total immersionists could fight it out doctrinally and forensically from two friendly pulpits. A cardinal Baptist belief had always been that a person has the right to private interpretation of the Bible and does not have to prate the theological directives of some would-be scholar or ecclesiastical big wig. By the same token, the Methodists were not going to be told by the Baptists that they could not baptize their own babies according to the scriptures, which drained many Methodists from the Sand Hill community. Bible interpretation was serious business, and spiritual food was a necessity. But so, too, was physical food—and Bedias had a general store.

The Bedias general store followed the pattern of its day. The customer first hitched his horse or team to a rail and entered the long, shotgun building through swinging doors. He found himself at the beginning of a wide-center aisle, which divided the sales counters that ran the length of the room. Groceries were kept on one side, dry goods on the other. Under the grocery counter were barrels of sugar, rice, beans, flour, and other staples. The top of the counter displayed a row of showcases, each about one foot square. Among other things, these boxes held a multicolored line of hard candies, some of which looked like chunks of glass. There were amber-colored horehound drops, leather-tough licorice sticks, and striped wands of peppermint, which the proprietor carefully sacked for the young fry when their fathers paid the bill.

At the back of the store, a connecting room held rows of home-cured hams and bacon, hanging on hooks, greasy barrels of lard, each with its wooden paddle, and other barrels of salt, vinegar, and coal oil (kerosene). The vinegar was sucked out of a barrel with a wooden pump and spewed into the customer's bottle or jug. The coal oil was in a horizontal barrel resting on X-trestles. It had a spigot on one end from which the merchant drained the kerosene into a can furnished by the customer. As soon as the can was filled, the storekeeper slapped a potato on its sharp spout so the precious fluid wouldn't slosh out on the bouncy trip home in the bed of the wagon.

Across the back of the main store was a long rack suspended

from the ceiling, displaying an assortment of buggy whips. There were also businesslike bull whips guaranteed to make a mule a little less stubborn and leather traps, horse collars, bridles, and all the accoutrement of the well-appointed surrey or farm wagon. Near this rack, on the last ten feet of the counter, was a series of holes of varying sizes. From each of them protruded a piece of hemp rope unwound on coils beneath. The customer simply pulled out the length of rope needed (as measured on a fixed rule on the counter's edge) and whacked it off with a razor-sharp knife convenient to his purpose.

The Bedias General Store was much more than a dispenser of the necessities of life. It was a social institution, a sort of public forum, a town meeting hall. Everybody came to town on Saturday and lingered on into the night. The men came into the store smelling of witch hazel and bay rum. They had been freshly shaved at the barber shop, after a week of whiskers.

People came for beans and flour, but first, conversation. By the old black stove, the weather and crops were prognosticated, politics was argued, and the timeless question of whether or not the whole darn country was going to the dogs was kicked about. At the back of the store, the women sat primly on benches, fanning themselves daintily while they discussed the latest in bustles and babies.

Bedias also had a post office. Mail arrived a little late in the back of a wagon from Huntsville or Navasota, some 30 miles away on the railroad. The first postmaster was Paschol H. Wilkinson. He drew no salary, but the prestige was enormous. In 1869, the Post Office Department set up a salary of $10 per month for the postmaster of Bedias, Texas, but Paschol had no such lucrative position on the government payroll. He did not mind. After all, he was postmaster. That was remuneration enough. Hardy men throughout rural America rode endless hours through mud, dust, and snow delivering the mail to outlying districts. In 1909, the salary of such carriers was raised to $30 per month.

What Bedias needed most was a railroad. Officials of the International and Great Northern Railroad were of the same opinion. Surveys were run across Sand Hill, Bedias, and

Fankey while interested citizens watched the progress with varying shades of jubilation. They knew that the railroad was of tremendous significance to the settlements through which it ran. Actually, when the rails were laid, they missed all three communities at first.

Incognito, in the guise of the Smith Land and Implement Company, the I. and G.N. bought a post-oak cow pasture from J. H. McKeown for a few dollars per acre. A whole townsite was laid out with street names, which some of the old-timers could not even pronounce—names of railroad officials. Lots were offered at what were then fantastic prices. Pioneers who had cleared the land half a century earlier—so a railroad might eventually extend its tracks to it—were ignored in the nomenclature of the streets.

The new town, under the hill from Bedias to the east, would have been the kiss of death to the old village had matters run their course. But the progressive people of Bedias simply moved their whole town to the new site. Not only that, but many residents of Fankey (to the west) and Cotton (to the east) moved their residences and businesses to the "promised land" on the railroad. This was to be the new Bedias, but not easily.

The railroad, with the cooperation of the Post Office Department, named the new town Trice. Railroad officials wanted one of their number by the name of Trice honored by having a town named after him somewhere along the tracks. Without so much as consulting one old-timer, they put the business through. One morning, the residents of what they thought was Bedias awoke to see that on each end of the brand-new depot was a name they had never heard of: Trice, Texas.

The railroad hierarchy did not reckon on the kind of men and women who had hacked a town out of the virgin forest back in the early 1830s or on their descendants. A chamber of commerce would have tackled such a situation, but all Bedias had was a bunch of fighting-mad townsmen. They were enough. The morning after the new sign swung for the first time in the breeze, news somehow leaked out that a group of high echelon railroad officials had left Navasota by special car to inspect the new town of Trice and its railroad facilities. The special car was not scheduled to stop, but it did.

Local residents turned a switch, shunting the train into a spur and ramming it into a box car. Part of the group boarded the car and pounded on the door for admittance. At first they were refused, but finally—for the sake of good public relations—the railroad officials opened the door for a conference. While the conference was in session, another group of citizens, with ladders and axes, removed the hated sign "Trice" in splinters and erected a sign that said "Bedias, Texas," as it does today.

It was a great moment when the "Jenny" wheezed its maiden way across north Grimes County from Navasota through Anderson, Roans Prairie, Singleton, and Bedias to Madisonville. Two drug stores, two banks, two cotton gins, a millinery shop, numerous merchandising houses, and a restaurant sprung up in Bedias.

Most important of all, a modern school building was erected, and a high school curriculum was inaugurated. The school board imported a superintendent from Missouri named George W. Pendergraft. He held the post for five years. He was highly educated, a rigid disciplinarian, and a devout Methodist. He never lost an opportunity to urge boys and girls to live worth-while lives of dedicated achievement. The worst that was ever said about Pendergraft was that he was a "damn Yankee from Missouri," but even that was tolerated for the sake of what he was doing for the youth.

It was inevitable that the development of Bedias would drain off many of the leading families from the surrounding communities. This was true of Sand Hill and the Bracewell family. Barto moved his residence and blacksmith shop; his brothers Frank and Calvin became merchants. Only my father, "Buddy", and his family remained at the old home place farming.

I was restless. I had made the big decision. I was going to be a lawyer. This meant that I had to have the very best education I could possibly acquire. Word from my cousins about the new high school and its superintendent kindled in my heart a desire to attend. I had developed an avid taste for knowledge, and books were a continuous adventure to me. Higher education was beckoning.

The school was four miles away. Although I was willing to walk, my mother had a better idea: I could ride the family mule, old Lucy.

◆◆◆

Where There's a Will (Bedias High School)

ON A DREARY morning in early October 1907, Lucy delivered me to Bedias High School in a shower of mud. My heart began to race as I contemplated the man whose reputation for learning had spread across the countryside. Dismounting and tethering the mule, I headed for the front entrance of the sprawling clapboard building. I climbed the three steps which led to the vestibule and stepped inside. There—not three feet from me—stood a tall, scholarly-looking man with steel-rimmed glasses and a plump, matronly little woman—Professor Pendergraft and his wife, the school's Latin teacher.

In those days there was no state curriculum for schools. Each school system depended totally on the wisdom and pedagogical skill of its superintendent and teachers, and that's why a man like Pendergraft was so important. In a very real sense, Pendergraft was Bedias High School.

After much kindly probing, the school superintendent decided that he would try me out in the ninth or junior class, warning me that it would take hard work and strict application to my studies to keep that educational slot. My courses would be second year Algebra, Plane Geometry, English and Rhetoric, Ancient History, and second-year Latin. I had never studied Latin, but Professor Pendergraft promised that his wife would help me catch up. I stayed an extra hour after school every day and learned to conjugate Latin verbs. In three months I was abreast of the other members of my class.

Gradually, I became accepted into the more sophisticated school life of the larger town. My only difficulty came during a recess period one afternoon of the first week. Two nicknames had always aroused me to physical battle. One was "Red" and the other was "Spec." I did not know just why these appellations infuriated me so, but they did. I did have red hair and I did have freckles. They were nothing to be ashamed of, but all a fellow had to do to get his mouth full of freckled knuckle was to refer to the long-legged lad from Sand Hill as "Spec" or "Red."

The most popular game on the school ground was shinny. It consisted of knocking a tin can across a line using a knotted and crooked oak stick. Two sides were chosen and the field of battle was laid out. Before long, the game became exactly that—a battle. (A solid whack on the shin with the oak club was guaranteed not to produce a polite rejoinder.)

In the heat of the fray, two lads on the opposing team began to chide me, a gawky boy from Sand Hill.

"You missed it, Red."

"Try again, Spec."

I straightened up. My eye was no longer on the battered can, but on two tousled heads. Gripping my shinny club in both hands, I yelled, "Don't call me them names again, or I'll knock your heads clean to the Brazos River."

Not trusting myself, I flung my club down on the ground and stalked from the field. That was the last time any schoolmate called me by either of the hated handles.

It took me several weeks to live down this exhibition, but my schoolmates finally discovered that I was generally affable. I was invited to school parties. I was socially accepted.

One day, Mr. Pendergraft called me aside. Without preamble, he said, "I'm proud of you, lad. You have what it takes. My wife says that you are one of the best students she has ever had, and she is hard to please. She says that you have a keen mind and a strong will. Tell me, what are you going to make of yourself? What are you going to do when you leave Bedias High?"

The reply was quick as the snap of a steel trap. "I'm going to go to Texas University and study law."

The schoolmaster's dark Methodist eyes studied me deeply. "Tell me, lad," he said, "do you honestly think that you could conscientiously defend a man whom you know to be guilty of a crime?"

There it was again. It seemed like just about everybody thought that in order to be a lawyer you had to be a trickster, if not a downright crook.

"I believe that even a guilty man should have the right of proper defense," came the slow answer.

These were strange, wise words from a 15 year old, and Mr. Pendergraft was impressed.

"Listen, son, if you want to be a lawyer, be the best one that you can. Study the life of Abraham Lincoln. If you can't match him intellectually, then match him in integrity. Read the story of Henry Clay, of Webster, Calhoun, Patrick Henry. No matter which way the political winds blew, they stood straight, son. They stood straight."

Bedias High School, one of the best in the area, was a far cry from the high schools of our day, even those in outlying sections. Each teacher carried the extremely heavy workload of two full grades. Equipment was poor. Modern facilities such as a laboratory, a gymnasium, and a cafeteria were nonexistent. A student was paid $10 per month to sweep the building, brush the furniture and make the fires in the huge, old, wood-burning stoves. Worst of all, the school had no library. But Mr. Pendergraft loaned me the books he recommended himself. The kindly superintendent had underlined the sentences and paragraphs he considered most important.

Occasionally, there were penciled notes beside the text; I valued these as much as I did the original content of the volumes. By the side of Lincoln's Gettysburg Address, Mr. Pendergraft had noted: "The most exalted writing by any mortal men." Beside Lincoln's stirring peroration—"and that government of the people, by the people, and for the people shall not perish from the earth"—was: "That's telling them, Abe. Great. True." Gradually I became permeated with the ideas of Pendergraft, who was more than a little left of center in his political ideology.

Since I was not very socially inclined, I had time to con-centrate on a difficult study program. My work allotment for my senior year consisted of Trigonometry, Solid Geometry and Physics, third-year Latin, English history, and both English and

American Literature. By the time he graduated, a student of Bedias High was conversant with the works of Shakespeare, Milton, Tennyson, Gray, Scott, DeQuincy, Bryant, Whittier, and Hawthorn.

By my second, or senior year, I felt that I was a pretty fair scholar. Competition for class honors was keen, and though I was selected as valedictorian, I did not come by the honor easily. The runner-up later became a distinguished dental surgeon.

On graduation night, I dressed in brand-new clothes, sat in cross legged dignity on the platform by the side of Superintendent Pendergraft. The proudest parents out front were Buddy and Mollie Bracewell as I stood to my feet and strode purposefully to the speaker's stand to give my valedictory address. My topic was "Socialism." In later life, I would defend more conservative political positions with greater persuasive skill, but never with more earnest enthusiasm.

◆◆◆

My First Date

Lucy played an important part in my first date. That was not the girl's name, but it was the name of the little mouse-colored mule which was my sole means of transportation. I'll call the girl "Jenny," but that was not her name either. She married another man soon thereafter, one with a chestnut sorrel mare and a beautiful, red-wheeled buggy. They reared a splendid family and would probably just as soon not get their names mixed up in this narrative.

JENNY HAD A wonderfully understanding mother, but the managing partner of the household was a pretty tough-looking cookie to a 16 year old. He looked much like Daniel Boone, although I must confess I didn't see any knives hanging from his belt; neither did he wear a coonskin cap. To me, it was quite interesting to speculate on how he would react to someone calling on his daughter. The fact that it was mid-July and two o'clock in the afternoon seemed to be in my favor.

The house sat back in the pasture about a half mile from the road. The front acreage was a woods where stock ranged— the cultivated fields were in the rear. The house was a large, double-pen structure with the parlor fenced off from the other rooms by a wide hall. It was quite well adapted to "sparking" if there only had been anything to talk about.

I had debated the matter of an adventure into romance at some length. After all, I was 16 years old, and most boys my age were having dates. If I was to be a lawyer, I would have to follow precedent. Then there was the point of learning to surmount difficulties, learning to talk under adverse circumstances, and learning to find the proper approach. Every argument seemed to be in favor of calling on Jenny and none against it.

Kinfolks around the community had teased Jenny about me and me about her. We had exchanged meaningful glances at church. When she and her friends went out the door on one side of the church to get a cool drink from the cistern, I rushed out the door on the other side and would be drawing a bucket of water when they got there. Jenny was bound to have observed my energy and chivalry. In fact, I thought we had reached a pretty fair understanding without a date.

But I was beginning to have a growing concern about another matter. One boy in our community had gone away to business school and had come back considerably polished up. He took a job clerking and keeping books in one of the stores. He walked around with a pencil behind his ear and a bunch of keys dangling from his belt. It all gave him a lot of prestige. I had observed him talking to Jenny a time or two and could see in him a vicious rival. That was all the more reason why I should strike now and isolate him from Jenny the best I could.

One of my female cousins was quite a good friend of Jenny's, and it occurred to me that the most promising approach would be to get her to call for me and make the date. So I saddled Lucy and galloped the mile to my cousin's. It would be no easy job to reveal my romantic ambitions to her, and I felt myself getting quite nervous even on the ride over. I saw no one around. I knocked and there was no answer. I turned the knob and went through the unlocked door. The clock ticked loudly. My heart-beats were greatly accelerated. There was a large wall telephone at my cousin's. By the simple expedient of ringing a long and two shorts, I might get *her* (Jenny) and talk to her *myself.*

I slumped into a chair to think things over. I laid aside my Baptist tutelage long enough to curse my own cowardice. A man who later had courage to fight his way through Cumberland University, fight his way up in the legal profession, and fight the battles of the underdog was now trembling and cowering before a little powdered and perfumed individual whom he had not even seen that day. I seized the telephone crank and had rung the fateful long and two shorts before I realized what I'd done. The die was now cast.

The terrifying feminine "Hello" came almost immediately. It was her mother! "The Lord is surely on my side," I thought, "because it could have been the old man."

"Is Jenny there? Could I talk to her?" I mumbled. "Yes, but who is calling her?" I couldn't imagine why Jenny's mother asked that. "This is Searcy Bracewell," I said between swallows. I heard her call Jenny and tell her who was on the phone. I had now passed the point from which there was no return.

"Hello," Jenny said.

"Jenny, this is Searcy, and I wanted to know if it would be all right for me to come by there to see you." Awkward words, of course, but they got the job done.

"Yes, it will be all right," she said.

"Well, I'll be over," I said; and with a short "Goodbye" that was almost curt, I eased up the telephone receiver.

I slumped down in a chair again utterly exhausted. I began to think of all the things I could talk about and how I would behave. How far should I sit from her? How would she act in the parlor with no one there but me?

As I pondered these matters, it suddenly occurred to me

that I had not told Jenny what time I would be there. It was then two o'clock according to the wall clock which was tick-tocking away in the big, empty house. Calling her again seemed a possible breach of good manners, and, too, she might cancel her acceptance. If she were expecting me right away and I kept her waiting until 3:30, she might be offended, and I would kill off all chances of favor I had. There was only one sensible decision, and that was to go now and take my chances on things working out for the best.

So I mounted the old mule, Lucy, and jogged along for the mile to the pasture gate. Never did a mile seem so short. I made sure to fasten the gate behind me. (The Lord was still on my side, as we shall later see.) I negotiated the remaining half mile to the fence surrounding Jenny's yard and tied Lucy to a tree with my bridle reins. To put on an appearance of confidence and composure, I approached the house with quick, measured tread. Jenny met me at the parlor door and invited me in. Immediately, a feeling of great personal achievement came over me. I surveyed every detail. Jenny wore an embroidered shirtwaist and a black skirt, with a red bow of ribbon in her hair. The chairs had been placed about six feet apart, and I accepted that as the conventional distance.

Conversation got under way. First, the weather got a good going over. It was getting quite warm, but I was sure it would soon be getting quite a bit warmer. Since we had considerable rain over our way, the crops were growing well and the crabgrass would soon be getting out of hand. The rain also was making the mosquitoes very bad.

Then we reviewed the events of the high school session and the inimitable qualities of Mr. Pendergraft. The growth of Bedias and all of the people who were moving there from Sand Hill and Mount Pleasant received due attention, as did the church and the singing school, which was to be held late in the summer, and the approaching box supper, which was to be staged at the Sand Hill School. In addition, we talked about the revival meeting to be conducted at the church under the leadership of Dr. McClung.

Finally, I guessed that it was about 3:30 p.m., and the initial date shouldn't be too long. It didn't seem that I had done so badly. The conversation, if not exactly amorous, had been quite informative. My composure had been completely restored. There had been a most respectful non-interference by the parental segment of the family. They knew of my intention to study law and who could tell whether they might not be debating whether it might be better to have a lawyer than a bookkeeper in the family.

And so with such musings, I managed to terminate the visit. After telling Jenny I had enjoyed myself and hoped to see her again soon, I began the same quick, measured tread through the yard gate and to the tree where I had hitched Lucy. I was in such a spirit of ecstasy about it all that I got almost to the tree itself before I noticed that it had nothing on it but an empty bridle.

Never were chagrin and frustration more complete. Riding a mule to see a girl wasn't in the best taste to begin with, but having to chase the mule over the pasture and maybe call for help before I could get home was the most bitter dregs of humiliation. If the bridle and reins had been a rope, I probably would have hanged myself to the first suitable tree I found. It would have been a welcome relief from my suffering. I felt that Jenny and, probably, her parents were watching me through the window, but I didn't look back. If their emotions were of pity, that would be even worse than ridicule would have been.

Lucy probably had been suffering more from the heat tied to a tree on the outside than I had been perspiring and palmetto fanning on the inside. At any rate, I figured that she would make a beeline for home three miles away as fast as she could get there. I made it on foot down to the pasture gate and found it still securely fastened. I then reasoned that the mule must have followed the fence to the right or left—looking for some gate or gap that she might slip through and get on her way home. I decided to follow the left side, extending nearly a mile through the woods, on the chance that I might find her roaming the fence.

But what would I do if I found Lucy? I probably couldn't catch her. What if I had to chase her to Jenny's house and have Jenny

and her family pen her? Well, if it took that, I just couldn't take it!
A thousand such thoughts raced through my feverish brain as I
trudged up the pathway along the fence. All of a sudden, I
heard the flapping of saddle stirrups, and here she came at a
high gallop. I hollered, "Lucy! Lucy! Lucy!" If I had any doubt
about the efficacy of prayer, it was completely dispelled by
what happened. Lucy slowed to a walk and approached me with
her head stuck out for the bridle. It was as if some great catas-
trophe had been miraculously averted.

Although the saddle blanket was gone, what did that
matter? I tightened the girth, mounted, and slowly made it
back with a feeling of thankfulness and humility. My emotions
had been so agitated for four hours that I felt numb. I passed
through the gate and turned left to ride on the opposite side of
the fence I had walked with such troubled spirits. I rode about
two miles to a friend's house and found he was not at home. I
then rode slowly back along the fence to view once more from
afar the scene of my triumph and humiliation.

As I turned the corner, I saw moving up the hill toward the
gate a two-horse buggy in which was seated my bookkeeper
rival. It was evident that he had phoned Jenny for a date after
I had left in pursuit of Lucy. It was further evident that he was
going to give Jenny a twilight ride in a two-horse buggy.

On my somber ride home, I did some soul searching. Surely,
the Lord never intended me to move in the social world until I
had proven myself in other fields. My first attempt had ended
in defeat and well-nigh disgrace.

◆◆◆

Chapter 2

Youthful Recollections

Lessons in Life

For me, the road to the Texas Bar was anything but smooth. My first setback came when I discovered that the merchants, bankers, and tradesmen of Bedias were unimpressed by either my diploma or by my strong right arm. I needed money in order to enter the University of Texas in the fall, but if there were any jobs available, I could not find them. I decided to look elsewhere.

Down San Antonio way it was customary to observe April 21, San Jacinto Day, with a big parade and other goings on. The railroad had an excursion rate. Why not go to see the Battle of Flowers and look for a good job in San Antonio? Besides, I had never been to a big city (San Antonio was nearly 100,000), and I wanted to get the feel of the world.

Buddy and Mollie concurred. Their son was now 17—almost a man. They were proud of this tall, red-haired product of their lives, and they loved me completely. They wanted me to have my chance. They were together when Buddy handed me $20—every cent they had.

I wanted to laugh and cry at the same time. Suddenly, I knew that the tender cord which linked childhood with parent-hood was being broken. Mollie was so frail. Her health was failing. I looked at my mother worshipfully. She was one more reason I had to make good. I wanted to be able to provide for her every need—and Buddy's. It was hard to believe, but my father was beginning to show signs of weariness, too.

The usual throngs were at the depot when the train wheezed into the block. The people stood proudly along the tracks as rotund, jolly Captain Jack took out his turnip-like watch, gave it a carefully-calculated glance and yelled, "All aboard!" As the engine screeched and puffed while the drivers gained traction, I settled myself in the horsehair seat and watched the fence rows crawl by the soot-blackened window.

The train was dirty and slow, stopping for coal and water frequently and then wheezing on into the placid countryside. Drummers played dominoes in the smoker, and every 30 minutes or so the butcher boy came through with a cry of "Get your apples, oranges, popcorn and candy, folks." His prices were twice the going rate in town. I had never been on a train before, and I was fascinated.

"San Antonio," Captain Jack said, punching the ticket.

San Antonio. The ghosts of Travis, Bowie, Bonham, and Crockett walked the streets. Across from the brick depot, the dingy sign of a rooming house swung lazily in the breeze. I shoved through the door and paid for a night's lodging—75 cents. I climbed the rickety stairway, let myself in and stood looking around. The bed was a brass-trimmed affair with a soggy mattress covered with a brownish bedspread with burned spots here and there. A washstand was in the corner with a speckled, cracked mirror above it. A porcelain pitcher of water stood in a porcelain basin.

Three long days later the Battle of Flowers was just a memory, and my hopes were beginning to fade. San Antonio seemed to be as jobless as Bedias.

The hotel desk clerk said that one of the regulars at the old Buckhorn Saloon might know of work. The Buckhorn was an Alamo City institution and the most democratic spot in town. Just about everybody went there except women. I wasted no time once inside the smoke-filled room. I spotted a jovial, flamboyant man with a big cigar. I stepped up and with a confidence that was wholly synthetic said, "Pardon me, mister. You seem to be a man who knows his way around. Could you tell a fellow where he might get a job in this city?"

The big man suggested I try the streetcar company, which was looking for motormen. Its offices, he said, were at the car barn.

I filled out an application for a job as a motorman. All seemed well until the personnel man asked my age—17. Motormen had to be 21.

San Antonio might be out, but I wasn't heading back to Bedias. I decided to try Sinton. It was only about 100 miles south in San Patricio County, and I had heard that it was booming. A druggist from Bedias who had gone there had sent back glowing reports of the town's enterprise.

When I inquired at the railway station, I found that the fare to Sinton and my cash on hand would just about come to balance. I hastened back to the rooming house and packed my large buckram suitcase, known in that day as a "telescope" because of its expandable nature.

Sinton was booming, all right, but there was no great demand for recent high school graduates. Eighty percent of the employed population were Mexican laborers working for a pittance. When I had almost given up, I found a job with a shingling crew at $2.50 per day. Room and board were $1.00, which gave me a net profit of $1.50 for ten hours of work on a hot roof under a tropical sun. Ten days of this and the young house shingler decided that there surely must be a better way of earning money. What about punching cows?

San Patricio and the surrounding counties were ranch and cattle county. That night, in my decrepit rooming house, I began to spin tales in my mind of the romantic life of the cowboy. I wound up not breaking broncs, but breaking my own back—pulling onions.

After paying the rooming house, I had $10 left. It was 40 miles to Runge, the center of the cattle country. I decided to ride the rails—hop a freight. Riding a freight as a dead-head was against the railroad company rules, but for 50 cents or a dollar, a brakeman could always be bribed and itinerant job-seekers, of whom there were hundreds roaming the country, could slip into the empty boxcars and bounce their way toward "Opportunity."

But when I got to Runge, I found that it and the surrounding territory had more cowboys than it needed.

Disconsolate to the point of tears, I bumped into Oscar Barnes, a cousin whom I had not seen in years. Oscar was an onion grower, and the season was in full swing. The onions were pulled from the ground by Mexican laborers paid 60 cents a day. Since I was a blood relative, Oscar offered to throw in room and board. It was the only job available, and the prospective lawyer took it with as much grace as I could summon. Oscar and I set off from town to the farm in a rickety, old hack drawn by a donkey.

There are many back-breaking jobs on a farm, but the epitome of all bad jobs must surely be pulling onions for market. The onions on this farm were large, as big as a man's fist, and grew close together on rows a "mile" long. The onion laborer crawled on my knees between the narrow rows, pulling the onions from the clinging soil, shaking them, and throwing them to either side. It took half a day to make a round trip. At least the monotony of the task gave me time to think. My first thoughts had to do with how to get away from that place.

At 60 cents a day, I would have to pull up onions from a row long enough to reach China before I could ever get to the university, I reflected. By that time my back would be permanently bent! How could a lawyer ever face a jury if he was so hump-backed he could only see his shoes?

After one week, I was riding the rails to Yoakum. Surely in a town of 8,000 there would be easier jobs then pulling onions. There may have been, but I never found one.

Where now? Back to the farm? It seemed to be the only hope. Taylor was the nearest town in the black land cotton country. After a night spent in a rundown, bedbug-ridden hotel, I made my way down to the railroad tracks. I immediately ran into trouble in the shape of a huge, red-faced Irishman who wore a badge and a gun. I had to dip into my meager store of cash for a ticket to Taylor.

Eventually, the train lurched into Flatonia—little more than a whistle-stop. Passengers bound for Taylor and other points in that direction had to change trains here. They also had to wait several hours for their next transportation. While I waited, I met a big man traveling with two youths my age. They'd been on the train from Yoakum. The man, a Mr. Stockton from Bartlett, announced that he was a cotton farmer looking for hands, and he offered me a job—$1.50 a day plus room and board. He even said he'd pay for the ticket to Bartlett. I accepted eagerly.

The old Stockton home was a colonial mansion. Mrs. Stockton, a bosomy, motherly woman, welcomed the three young men with a warmth which made them a little homesick, and she proved to be one of the best cooks in Texas.

The cotton chopping lasted about a month. Once the crops were laid by, there was nothing else for the boys to do. I had by then accumulated a bankroll of between $30 and $40. It was about two months before the university opened. Mr. Stockton suggested I try looking for work in Waco.

Businessmen in Waco were as unimpressed by my high school diploma as those in Bedias, San Antonio, Sinton, and Yoakum had been. There wasn't even any farm work to be had.

By now I was as familiar with the inside of a railroad station as I was with the palm of my calloused hand. It was a sort of refuge for me while I assembled my thoughts. At the Waco station I saw a sign: "Butcher Boy Wanted." (Back in those days, each train had a butcher boy who passed through the car selling candy, cookies, etc.)

I had seen the butcher boys those days when I was making like a moneyed man, riding the cushions—the passenger cars. Within 30 minutes I had signed up for the job. My run was on the Texas Pacific from Waco west to Rotan in Nolan County— a frontier territory just opening up. It was a night trip, but I did not mind staying up all night if I could make a little money. The only trouble was that while I might stay awake all night, everybody else on the train would be sound asleep, and there would be no kids yelling for candy or adults wanting newspapers. I was forced to put up $15 bond to insure that I would return any merchandise I didn't sell. I rented a blue suit with shiny brass buttons and a blue cap to match and with a wobbly sort of dignity began my new job.

After two runs to Rotan, I knew that I was a loser, but I did not know how much of one. When I tried to check out of the job, the agents insisted that I was $13 short between the merchandise on hand and my receipts. Either that merchandise had been stolen or I had been swindled by the agents—not an uncommon practice. Of my $15 deposit, I received $2.

A less stout-hearted young man would have given up then and gone back to Bedias. After my butcher boy experience, I had $20 left—what I had when I left home. As I walked around the depot trying to decide what to do next, a newspaper lying on a set caught my eye. The want ads! It was strange that I had not thought of them before. Eagerly, I began scanning the five-point type. Here was something: "Wanted. Sawmill Workers. Good Wages." It gave Trinidad over in Henderson County as the place of employment. Should I try for a freight or ride the cushions? After my experience in the blue uniform, it just didn't seem right somehow to ride the rails. I plunked down the cash for a ticket.

Two other youths about my age were waiting for the train, and I struck up a conversation with them. They were on their way to Trinidad for jobs with the same lumber company. It was only after they had climbed aboard the train that I learned that the lumber company had paid their fares. I could have saved $3 had I known in time.

In due course, the train pulled into Trinidad, a swampy railroad crossing with very few houses. The sawmill was two miles out, and the only transportation was our feet. Off we three went in the July heat, lugging our unwieldy telescope suitcases. We arrived at noon, just as the hands were filing into the mess hall to eat. We registered at the office and were told to go over and eat, and we could go right to work.

In darkest Russia there probably was no slave camp that was more loathsome than this lumbering layout. Every man looked anemic or as though he had just gotten over a siege of typhoid fever. The flies and filth were almost unbelievable. Although I had not been a quitter up to now, this was just too much. The other lads who had come into camp with me felt the same way. The older of them, Bill Osgood, offered a suggestion.

He had heard that the peach and tomato crops were good around Jacksonville in Cherokee County.

Ten minutes later, we were back on the stumpy, muddy road, lugging our "telescopes" and grumbling at the heat. But such is the buoyancy of youth, and such is its strength, that the prospects of adventure outweigh everything else. In about 45 minutes, the three disappointed mill hands arrived back at the depot. We had decided to try for a freight before putting out any more money. As it turned out we got a ride, all right—but to jail.

A large, big-hatted man with a shotgun asked if we weren't Jim Thomas, Bill Osgood, and Searcy Bracewell. Then—without explanation—he carted us off to the lockup in Athens, the county seat. In about two hours, the county attorney showed up. Only then did we learn of the charge against us. It was suspicion of fraud. The lumber mill had complained that we had accepted company transportation money to Trinidad but had walked off the job before even going to work. I protested that I had paid my own fare.

We poured out our story to the lawyer, a young man of evident good breeding. He believed us and ordered us released immediately. Deciding to stick together in our search for work, we headed for Jacksonville, but it was the same old scratchy, broken gramophone record: no work. Beaumont was next. We got jobs near there sure enough—high-powered jobs. We hired out to a dynamite factory. The pay was a whopping $2.50 a day and board. This was the biggest money we had a chance to earn.

The making of dynamite was a relatively simple process, except when something went wrong. One crew mixed nitroglycerin with sawdust. The resultant mixture was stockpiled and conveyed down to hoppers by a small van. Each rookie workman—like the three of us—was responsible for one hopper. The hopper was filled with the mix, which the workmen tapped into a cardboard cylinder about an inch in diameter and 15 inches long, pressing it into the tube with a piece of steel, like stuffing sausages.

After two weeks, I told my two friends good-bye. It was the middle of August, and cotton was beginning to open around

Bedias. I could go home, pick cotton for a couple of weeks or more, and then be ready to enter the University of Texas.

Three months after I had left Bedias seeking work, I returned. I had $20 in my pocket—exactly the amount with which I had ventured into the outside world. All that I had to show for the three months was experience.

I went to work picking cotton for Carson Wells, a devout and good man interested in all young men who were seeking an education. Then, one day I told my kindly employer of my plans to become a lawyer.

"A lawyer!" exclaimed Mr. Wells. "How can a God-fearing man adopt such a profession? How can he defend a man who is guilty?"

Mr. Wells became so upset that I might have lost my job had the cotton not been opening so fast and had it not been so difficult to get pickers so early in the season.

Finally, it was time to go to school. A Bedias physician, Dr. Barnes, advised me to go on to Austin and enroll in the university and then try to get work for my room and board. The good-hearted doctor promised to keep a financial lifeline open so that I could hang on until I got adequate work.

Then came the crowning disappointment of them all. I was unable to enter Texas University. My beloved alma mater, Bedias High School, was unaccredited. My diploma was worthless at the university. I had only one chance. I could take the entrance examination in the hope that my score would be high enough to permit my enrollment. I tried it. Most of the questions were about subjects in which I was wholly ignorant. The registrar informed me that I had failed.

Now, at long last, I felt my determination breaking. I walked around the campus for several hours in a complete daze.

What now? Out of the dim past I seemed to hear again the words of my high school principal. "Remember one thing about Abraham Lincoln, Searcy. He never gave up."

I went back to Mr. Stockton, who gave me a job as overseer of a farm near Temple. I was to take complete charge, weighing and keeping records of the cotton, carrying it to the gin, marketing the crop, and putting the money in the bank. The

pay was $2.50 per day with room and board. The biggest thrill
of all came when Mr. Stockton took me to Temple, about 30
miles away, in his brand-new automobile. This was such an
exhilarating experience that I forgot—for a little while—my
extreme disappointment in not getting into the university.

I arrived back in Bedias at Christmas time with a total of
nearly $100 in my pocket. I took odd jobs around town until
spring. In the meantime, I had learned that I could attend
Jacksonville Baptist College at a cost of $7 per month and no
tuition. This caused great rejoicing among my kinfolk
and acquaintances in Mount Pleasant. They were certain in
their own minds that I was giving up my hair-brained idea of
becoming a lawyer and would be a preacher instead. The pay
might not be much, but at least the job was respectable.

◆◆◆

The Back Door to the Texas Bar

I WAS NOT quite 18 years of age. I reasoned that if I could
attend Jacksonville College for a year and get a teacher's
certificate, I could earn enough money in about two years to go
to the university. By that time, I would be 21 and could enter
on individual approval.

There were about 150 students enrolled in Jacksonville
College, and some 50 of them were over 17 years of age.
They were all from good families, extremely devoted to the
principles out of which the Baptist Missionary Asociation
(BMA) grew. All went to church twice every Sunday and sat
under the preaching of Dr. J. N. Newburn, one of the
outstanding pulpiteers of his time. Many of Dr. Newburn's
ideas made their way into my later writings. I owe men like
Newburn more than I could repay in a dozen lifetimes.

The ghost of J. Werner Hoppe also appeared in many courtroom dramas as I pled my cases. Dr. Hoppe was a past master in
the dramatic art of reading. This unusual man could seemingly
memorize an entire book overnight and be ready to present it

almost with the vividness of color television. The genius of the immortal Bard of Avon lived as Hoppe recited a stirring dialogue from "Hamlet," taking both parts.

Something else grew out of the year at Jacksonville College—my knowledge of and love for preachers of the gospel. Since this was largely a preacher-training school, my classmates were—in the main—young theologues. No one knew better than I that the pastor of a church, no matter how large or small, was still just a man, with a man's weaknesses and need of understanding. From my college days until the end of my life, I was a friend to preachers.

My virility and enthusiasm made me somewhat of a favorite with the student body. Gone forever was the shyness with which I had entered high school. I was beginning to find myself.

FRANK MEAD'S *Handbook of Denominations in the United States* lists 260 religious bodies. Of these, 26 bear the name "Baptist." They ranged from the giant Southern Baptist Convention with its 11,000,000 members—the largest non-Catholic denomination in America—to the "Two-Seed-in-the-Spirit-Predestinarian Baptists," with about 200 members in fewer than twenty churches. Southern Baptist state conventions have undergone schisms in several areas. This happened to the Texas state convention around the turn of the century. This bitter division grew out of a difference in opinion about a procedural matter rather than from a dispute about basic interpretation of scripture.

Out of this particular controversy came a lawsuit which is more or less famous in the legal archives of Texas. Dr. A. A. Hayden sued Dr. J. B. Gambrell, Dr. J. B. Crenfill—and five or six other leaders of the Southern Baptist Convention—for slanderous remarks alleged to have been made by the committee which was considering the controversial questions.

After a fierce court fight, Dr. Hayden—who was editor of the influential paper *The Texas Baptist*—recovered from Drs.

Gambrell and Crenfill $10,000 in actual damages and $5,000 in exemplary (spite) damages. The case was appealed to the Court of Civil Appeals where it was affirmed (*Cranfill v. Hayden*, 75 S.W. 573 (Tex. Civ. App. 1903)), but a writ of error was granted, and the Supreme Court reversed the decision on the account of the inadmissibility of some of the evidence introduced. (*Cranfill v. Hayden*, 97 Tex. 544, 80 S.W. 609 (Tex. 1904)).

Baptists throughout Texas began to take sides. Those who were partisans of Dr. Hayden became known as Haydenites, and the followers of Crenfill and Gambrell were called the Board Party. Later, the dissenting group took the name "Baptist Missionary Association," which they hold to this day.

The members of Mount Pleasant Baptist Church—to which all of my people belonged—sided with the Hayden faction and became violent partisans. Since the large majority of the convention—when the division came—was the Board Party, it naturally became the possessor of all the property of that corporate body. This included its church schools and, particularly, Baylor University.

The Haydenites, or Church Party, had to start from scratch; but they went out with unrelenting zeal, and what they lacked in material resources they made up for in determination. Many of the churches which became affiliated with the Baptist Missionary Association were located in East Texas, Arkansas, and Louisiana. One of the first concerns of the new convention was the establishment of a college to train young preachers to serve those churches.

Jacksonville—a town in a part of Texas almost fantastic in its beauty and noted for its production of cotton, peaches, and tomatoes—was selected as a site for such a school. The 15-acre campus lay on an elevation behind the Cottonbelt Railroad. A three-story building, with a spire visible for miles, was erected on the hill.

Dr. J. N. Newburn, pastor of the First Baptist Church of Jacksonville, became one of the directing heads of the college and its principal promoter. His large, 12-room frame residence adjacent to the campus became the girls' dormitory. Dr. J. V. Vermillion, also one of the leading pastors in the area, became president of the new college. He, too, lived next to the campus, and his house became the boys' dorm. The Collins and Allbritton families were prominent in Jacksonville and were also denominational leaders. From their ranks came instructors, a post also filled by Mrs. J. V. Vermillion, the charming and dedicated wife of the president and hostess of the boys' dormitory.

Staff members were selected more for their consecration to God's cause and their willingness to work for little or no salary than for their experience and training as educators. However, there were two members of the faculty who had been teachers, and in later life distinguished themselves as educators: J. Werner Hoppe and Marvin Rushing. By the time I entered in 1910, the college had been in existence four or five years.

Jacksonville Baptist College had been widely advertised among the BMA Baptists as a place where an education could be obtained on a most economical basis, where a proper spiritual life could be developed, and, particularly, where preachers could be educated and trained in true principles of Baptist beliefs, policy, and practice. By reason of the fruit and vegetable productivity of the area, young men and women were boarded at nominal cost, as little as $7 or $8 per month.

Jacksonville College had then, and still has, a debating society in which practically the entire student body took part. "That was right up my alley," I said later. "Why, I even got elected president at the beginning of the second semester."

I was nominated to this post by G. E. Ellis, who became a noted preacher in subsequent years. In his nominating speech, my enthusiastic classmate predicted that I would become a great statesman and needed to be trained in the art of handling such organizations, since he would in time be presiding over large political conventions.

Though a school like Jacksonville Baptist College would rate sub-zero academically today, no single year in my life brought more benefit to my mind and personality than my stay at the little Baptist institution in East Texas.

Schools like Jacksonville College, fighting for survival in comparative obscurity, are integral to the best of the American

scene. Out of the very class to which I belonged came several
eminent ministers and educators. The college still operates,
but has yet to qualify for accreditation.

◆◆◆

From Sam Houston State Teachers' College to Roans Prairie School Principal

IN THE SPRING of 1910, about two months before school was
out, I left Jacksonville Baptist College.

Two considerations prompted my action. First, my money
ran out. True, I might have found some little employment to
get me through 60 days, but I felt that it would be a waste of
money.

Internal dissension at the college was the prime motivating
influence in my decision. Dr. J. V. Vermillion had become a very
unpopular man with the students. Some of his personal habits
had caused criticism, and his mental attitudes left much to be
desired. He was irritable, dogmatic, and—the students felt—
unfair. They staged a sit-down strike in order to rid the
college—and themselves—of the president. The maneuver
failed. The morale of the student body sank until just being at
the institution was taxing on the nerves. Learning was out of
the question.

My impulse left me faced with a problem which had to be
solved. If I persisted in my desire to enter law school, I would
need money—enough to see me through so I could apply
myself properly to my studies. The only solution was to teach
school for two or three years, but Jacksonville College had no
accreditation, and I had not finished the courses there anyway.

The answer to my problem was Sam Houston State
Teachers' College at Huntsville, some 30 miles from my
home town. I could go to summer school and get a teaching
certificate and be qualified to hold a position which would earn
enough to make law school more than a nebulous dream. But
even one summer at Sam Houston College cost money.

I got a job on a farm—the kind of work I knew best—and to which my physical stamina adapted me. During April and May, I did some of the hardest work of my life and denied myself every pleasure which cost any money whatsoever. I ended up with almost $30; I needed more.

I turned to my friend, Dr. Luther Barnes of Bedias. While Dr. Barnes didn't think much of lawyers, he admired my determination and lent me the money, joking that he expected me to defend him if he were ever sued for malpractice.

In June, I entered Sam Houston State Teachers' College. Since my sole purpose was to pass the state teacher's examination, I took only those subjects in which I felt I was the weakest. Agriculture had just been added to the curriculum and, although I had been born and raised on a farm, the book on agriculture offered to me was about as difficult as a volume on calculus or trigonometry. But, I reasoned if I was going to teach out of a book, I had better know exactly what the text said and, if possible, why. So I applied myself to the latest theories and methods of farming with a study of domestic and world markets thrown in. I also applied myself to mathematics on the assumption its study would help develop my reasoning powers.

Sam Houston State Teachers' College then had about 600 students from every corner of Texas. All were single. Students of both sexes seemed to have two supreme ambitions—the first was to get enough credits for a teacher's certificate without taking the examination, and the other (particularly among the girls) was to have a good time and get married as soon as possible after finishing school. I did not fit into either category. I was in dead earnest. I wanted to learn and—although teaching school was not my lifetime ambition—determined that while I taught I would give the best I had.

Huntsville is located about ten miles from Phelps, on the main line of the IGN Railroad from Houston to Palestine, but nothing more than a flag station in the piney woods of Walker County. The law at that time required all railroads to go through the county seat of any county they entered. In order to bypass Huntsville and still meet legal requirements, the IGN had a ten-mile tap line over which was shuttled a passenger car or two every time the regular passenger train came through.

Campus dormitories and cafeterias were unknown in that day. Huntsville was filled with boarding houses, each providing for between two and fifteen boys or girls. Most of the boarding houses were packed into the half-mile between the town square and College Hill. I stayed at the Mann House. There were eight other boys in the huge, old house operated by a very elegant widow who had a grown son of her own and was, thus, in touch with the problems of young men. She was sympathetic, encouraging, gracious and tender—without being overly solicitous. The other students were getting their certificates on credits issued by the college upon completion of certain courses but, as I said later, "I was the only maverick trying to get by on a state examination." Mrs. Mann knew this and gave a little extra attention to me.

After two perspiring months, the day of the examination finally rolled around. I felt that I was ready for it. In fact, I looked forward to it with a certain eagerness. I was no longer afraid of mathematics, but recognized my deficiency in agriculture and rhetoric. Sure enough, when I got the questions on these two subjects, I almost had a blackout. "What is osmosis?" I had never heard of it.

I struggled through the paper, but felt that my situation was so weak that daring strategy was warranted. At the bottom of my last sheet, I wrote boldly, "If you can conscientiously give me a passing grade on this subject, I think I can make it on the rest and have a sufficient general average for passing."

Aspiring teachers had to make a minimum of 50 on each subject and a general average of 75 in order to pass. About 30 days later, when the examination report came in, I found I had made at least 50 on each subject and had totalled an average of 76. Now, all that I had to do was get a position, save my money until I was ready to enter law school, delve a little into Clark's *Elementary Law* and apply myself to Blackstone's *Commentaries* while I waited to tackle my last educational battle before facing life in earnest.

Then came disappointment. All schools had already employed their teachers for the next year—my teacher's certificate had been issued too late for me to get a school to teach. I thought of my brother, Ernest, who was operating a small printing business and issuing a weekly newspaper in Shiro, *The Shiro Advertiser*. I headed for Shiro and prevailed upon my brother to give me a job—and I went to work as a printer's devil for my brother.

Reflecting on the course of events, it looks like Providence may have had a hand in my case. Two ladies, dressed most attractively, came to the office one day and wanted to contribute a few items of news from Roans Prairie for *The Shiro Advertiser* and place a small order for printing. Ernest introduced them to me as Mrs. Andrew Blount and Mrs. Robert Dreher and asked me to take the order. Each lady would have made a perfect example for study by Dr. Vermillion.

"Blount." I had heard of that name somewhere. A moment's reflection and I remembered that it was the name of an old East Texas pioneer family. Stephen W. Blount of San Augustine had presided over the Constitutional Convention which declared Texas independent. Eugene Blount of Nacogdoches was a friend of Governor Ferguson and at that time had a powerful influence in the Texas Legislature. It further occurred to me that Lucy Blount had become my Grandfather Shanks' second wife. I wondered if they might all be kin, but of course, asked no questions.

Type was set by the hand and stick method. The stick was a brass receptacle held in one hand to receive the type in column widths. This type was picked individually—a letter at a time—from boxes in a rack. Each letter shank was scored to indicate the right side for composition. An adept typesetter could turn out seven galleys a day. After two months, I could set two galleys in that time, so I never became a master of the art, but there were compensations—one of which was far-reaching in effect.

A few days later—while I was yearning for a chance to prove my skill as a school teacher and like a flash out of the blue—the news reached Shiro that the school principal in Roans Prairie had resigned and the position was open. I also discovered that a protracted revival meeting was soon to be held in the old Oakland Church in Roans Prairie. How did I know? I had set the type for the advertisements myself. All of a sudden, I began to feel evangelistic. If I attended services, maybe I would find out who the trustees of the school were. There were only two weeks until school started. I hired a horse and buggy and immediately drove the three miles over to Roans Prairie to see the trustees.

I went to the revival meeting. The church was crowded. But before and after the service, I did a good job of introducing myself and shaking hands. Here were Mrs. Blount and Mrs. Dreher who kindly remembered me as the red-haired, freckle-faced boy at the printing office. Each of the matrons had two daughters in tow, the older—in both cases—a pretty teenager. The Blount girls were Lola and Alma, and the Drehers were Ethel and Bobbie Merle.

At the revival I learned that the trustees of the Roans Prairie school were J. F. Hadley, one of the local merchants, and J. D. Phillips and Jim Mayfield, both farmers.

The next morning, I was at Mr. Hadley's store. He was modest, but specific about his qualifications to take charge of the school. Whether or not Mr. Hadley's decision was influenced by the fact that he and his wife were also running a boarding house and could furnish room and board to the incoming principal, I never knew. All I cared about was Mr. Hadley's assurance that he would endorse me for the school position if I could elicit the support of the other trustees. At that moment, the other school officials were picking cotton about a mile from the store and could be reached after a brisk walk though the adjoining pasture. The heat was 102° in the shade, and I had worked up a sweat by the time I reached the snow-white cotton field where Mayfield and Phillips were dragging their long sacks down the rows. I pitched in while I told them of my qualifications and desire to serve as school principal. I also casually mentioned that Mr. Hadley had promised his support.

Mayfield and Phillips authorized me to have the county school superintendent fill out the contract and send it to them for their signatures. Whether they were influenced more by sympathy for me in my eagerness to get the position or by the dire emergency of not having a principal on the job on the opening day of school, I never knew, but I was accepted and went back to Shiro in a very optimistic frame of mind.

It was just one week before school was scheduled to open.

I was pleased to learn that the salary of the principal was $65 per month, and that of one assistant was $50. I wondered how the school district could pay such magnificent salaries and remain solvent. For the first time since I had left Bedias High School, I really felt that I was on a self-sustaining basis. Due to my superior qualifications, I was certain that the duties of school principal would be easy enough for me to devote a good part of my time to Clark and Blackstone and their unravelling of the mysteries of jurisprudence. But I had a jolt coming.

The Hadleys provided room and board for $12.50 per month at a small hotel and rooming house where all the village news was gathered and disseminated—usually with some editing and elaboration. I learned that the school was regarded as a pretty tough one from the standpoint of discipline. A few bullies were said to be prone to take the school over and run it. This, together with the fact that the school was a little over my head at ten grades, gave me a feeling of lonesomeness. I felt quite susceptible to 'undue influence' from all the little kindnesses that might be shown me.

The operation of the school called for ten grades, four of which—the seventh through the tenth—were all taught by the principal. The first six grades were taught by the assistant or by the elementary teacher. The curriculum for the four grades which were my responsibility included second year Latin, Plane Geometry, Agriculture, Rhetoric, English, and American literature. Law would have to wait.

Roans Prairie was a most satisfactory community in which to live. The little town supported five substantial stores, a large cotton gin, a barber shop, and two hotels. For its size, it was blessed with a large number of young people between the ages of 17 and 20. The community was located on the IGN Railroad, about midway between Madisonville and Navasota. The passenger train went to Madisonville early in the afternoon and returned later in the day. This was the train that went through Bedias. It became the custom for everybody in town to meet the train twice a day, and if anybody missed doing so it was because of sickness or some other emergency.

The Monday after I was hired as principal—and unaware of the townspeople's habit—I stepped from the passenger coach and almost fled promptly back aboard. I had never seen so many people together in all my life. I had certainly never expected to see so many in a welcoming committee.

The next Monday school began. I had provided myself with a handbell and, at assembly time, I rang it with vigor and authority. After the preliminaries had been attended to, the principal made assignments for the following day. I soon saw that I was in trouble. School was out early that first day, but there were hundreds of details to be handled in person by the new master. Besides this, I had to prepare for teaching 16 subjects, many of them unfamiliar.

That night, I did not sleep at all. I studied until my head ached, my eyes hurt, and my back was sore. Some time in the middle of the night I resolved to go to the trustees in the morning and tell them that I had misrepresented my qualifications and would like to back out of the job as soon as I could.

Much to my surprise, the next day was not so bad. The third day of my tenure I began to relax. I learned to side step and cover up the things I did not know. By the end of the week, I was in the groove.

My first task was to make up a roll and become acquainted with the student body. I soon learned that there were two sets of sisters who were most attractive, admired and quite well raised—namely Lola and Alma Blount and Ethel and Robbie Merle Dreher. I immediately connected these girls with the two charming women I had met in the printing office. According to Dr. Vermillion, when these girls grew to advanced maturity, they would be beautiful women of fine sensibilities.

Of the four, Lola, age 15, was the oldest and assumed a natural leadership over the others. She was beautiful and quite gifted in her studies. She was in the ninth grade. I soon learned to rely upon her for information and help in the solution of my problems, which were many. I used her as a substitute teacher during my assistant's frequent absences.

Before long, I was getting compliments from the patrons of the school. Early in the term the county school superintendent, W. Stewart Barron, paid the Roans Prairie School a visit. He was quiet, with a scintillating mind and good personality. He and I liked each other on sight. Barron had legal ambitions, too. His every spare moment was spent in the study of law.

Thus began a lifetime friendship profitable to both. Barron had a distinguished career. He passed the state bar examination without difficulty, built up a good practice, was elected to the state legislature several times, and was speaker one term. He was then appointed district judge for Bryan and held that position many years.

At the end of my first year as principal, I was offered a renewal of the contract at $100 per month, accompanied by the suggestion that the trustees would favor a bond issue to replace the old frame building with a well-equipped one of brick. The offer was too attractive to turn down. Actually, it was three years before the new building was completed. I saw the project through, but never got to use the new structure. I resigned to study law. I had managed to save $500.

When it actually came time to leave Roans Prairie, I felt a tug at my heart. I felt that I had grown up in the little town. I now had a man's outlook. I could make a long-range plan and follow through. I had communicated with the firm of Dean, Humphrey and Powell in Huntsville and had been invited for an interview.

I became attached to the firm and found these older men warm-hearted and intelligent companions. One day Judge Powell suggested that I consider going to Lebanon Law School. Operated by the Presbyterian Church in Lebanon, Tennessee, it was a one-year school with one of the best records in the United States for getting its students by state bar examinations. The school's interest didn't stop there though. Its officials gave every assistance to the alumni in helping them with difficulties which they encountered in their law practices. From this school had come United States senators, governors, Supreme Court justices, district judges, and men successful in every phase of law.

I was convinced. As I prepared to leave for Tennessee, the newspapers flashed the headlines that Archduke Ferdinand of Austria had been assassinated. Two weeks before I left for law school, war was declared.

◆◆◆

"Mama-Lo"

DR. J. V. VERMILLION, president of Jacksonville Baptist College (which I attended one year), was an old-timer and was quite strong for the principle that the forces of heredity and environment exercise a powerful influence in shaping our lives. He had a habit of saying, "Young gentlemen, if you want to know what your future wife will look like 30 years from the time you marry her, just go take a good look at her mother, and you will have the answer." Those of us who have lived a long span of life will probably agree that the doctor had something there. Since all young men want their wives to remain attractive and a helpful yokefellow, what he said made a lasting impression on me.

I was at the Roans Prairie school three years. I visited in the Blount home and discerned that Mrs. Blount was not only an immaculate housekeeper, but a cook par excellence. These qualities didn't hurt as far as I was concerned. Mr. Blount was a hard-working, well-to-do farmer and cattle raiser. I learned that Lucy Blount, my grandfather's second wife, was his sister.

During the two years before Lola Blount finished high school, I formed a deep attachment for her. In fact, it grew into a passionate love. I had reason to believe she returned my feelings, but the proprieties of the occasion forbade any overt expression of them. Yet there seemed to be a great gulf between us. How was I to pass from teacher to suitor in a small community where gossip had long been practiced as one of the fine arts? My plight was further complicated by the fact that her beauty and charms were such that she had more suitors already than I cared to contemplate, and there seemed to be no way to compete with them.

Moreover, the whole idea of falling in love and getting married cut squarely across my lifelong purpose of becoming a lawyer. I had nurtured the thought too long to give it up easily. In those days, it was quite a feat for a young couple to go through the starvation period that a young lawyer endured, but to add to that a two or three-year period of study was beyond the range of possibility. I just couldn't give up the study of law and decided to let time reconcile the conflict if such a thing were possible. Maybe Lola would go to college. Then I could go to that town and study law and pass from teacher to suitor. But Mrs. Blount decided against her daughter going to college.

This decision seemed to be a little rough at the time, but the passing years have shown that it was probably wise and beneficial. The only avenue I could see left was to go ahead and study law somewhere and try to bridge the gap by correspondence. This I did.

One thing that made it a tough decision was that money was scarce. World War I was just beginning in full fury, and I knew I could not possibly come back to Roans Prairie until the expiration of the year's course. Since we were not engaged, I felt it would be presumptuous to talk to Lola about my plans. And, too, I reasoned that if I could weather the competition for an entire year wholly by correspondence, it would be a sign as sure as Moses had when he drew a leprous hand from his bosom that our union was the will of the Lord.

So Lola must have been quite bewildered when she received a letter from me from Lebanon, Tennessee, saying that I proposed to be gone a whole year to get a license to practice law. The promptness with which she answered the letter and her tolerant and sympathetic attitude toward my ambition to become a lawyer led me to hope that maybe after all it would not completely wreck my matrimonial aspirations.

Perhaps the sequence of events rendered Lola more diligent in preparing herself to take full part in such professional life as might be ahead for us. She joined several clubs of which she became president and in later years was designated Mother of the Year by the Fourth District of Women's Clubs in Texas. She taught a Sunday school class and headed all Sunday school departments from the cradle roll to adults. She read widely and made notes on everything. She knows more about flowers, trees, plants, birds, rocks, and missionaries than any other person I know. She traveled widely with me in the development of The Broadway Plan and is an accomplished traveler. She loves people, birds, cats, flowers and almost everything of which you can think. If being educated is acquiring the knack of being happy and getting along with people, she is one of the best educated people you could find—although she is without the benefit of college training.

Lola is not afraid of anything, but mice and snakes. When Fentress was to be sent overseas from Boston and I couldn't go along with her, she boarded a train (all plane space was reserved for soldiers) and went alone. She can sit up all night with the sick, watch people die, and dress a corpse.

I have a one-track mind. It is fairly good while it is on the track, but Lola is the most versatile person I have ever known.

Neither she nor Mrs. Blount wanted to be called "Grandma." Our sons, Searcy and Fentress, called Mrs. Blount "Mama" and Lola "Mother"; so when the grandchildren came along, there was a question of terminology. The grandchildren, of course, wanted to call their own mothers "Mother." When the oldest one got mature enough to talk, she boldly solved the difficulty by calling her grandmother "Mama-Lo." The name has stuck, and she is known as that by all the grandchildren—as well as by the children and others in the vicinity where she lived.

Path to Lebanon, Tennessee

THE WHEEZY STEAM engine belched a series of staccato coughs, and the drive wheels bit against the shiny rails. The brass-trimmed bell up the smokestack clanged authoritatively. I was off for Lebanon, Tennessee, nearly 1,000 jerky, smokey miles away. It was September 1, 1914—five years after I had reached up a prideful hand for my diploma from Bedias High. My heart was light.

Lebanon Law School had no entrance requirements, and students were expected to finish the course of studies in one 12-month period. Required books could be had for the modest rental price of a dollar per volume. "I've got it made!" I thought as I leaned back against the horse-hair cushions.

Just then the news butcher swayed down the aisle. "Huns march on Paris!" he cried.

Students bound for Phelps looked at each other soberly. After all, wars were fought by young men. I tried to put such somber thoughts in the background. I remembered with an unexplainable feeling of nostalgia the three months I had spent in the office of Messrs. Dean, Humphrey and Powell. Judge Powell had even promised money should the need arise.

I changed trains at Memphis about midnight. I swung aboard the L&N for Nashville and Lebanon, moving back to the uncrowded smoker so I could stretch out and sleep. Slumber overtook me almost as soon as I had given up my ticket, and I slept soundly until after Nashville. Then for some reason, I found myself wide awake.

Across the aisle was a big, white-hatted officer with a couple of huge revolvers strapped around his middle and two prisoners handcuffed together and to the seat.

"Howdy," said the big man. "Name's Northern."

"Mine's Bracewell—Searcy Bracewell."

"Which way you heading?" asked the officer in a friendly manner.

"On my way to Lebanon. Entering law school there."

"Great!" yelled the lawman. "I live there, and I'm taking these fellows back to answer for burglary and larceny committed in that county. Some cute lawyer will probably get 'em off the hook," he said meditatively. "Sometimes I think we have too darn many lawyers."

"I take it that you find it a little rough trying to enforce the law around the famous law school ..."

"I didn't mean it quite that way," shot back the other with a wide grin. He was an entirely different looking man with the good humor crinkles around his mouth. "I just mean that I have my two hands full."

I looked significantly at the large revolvers.

The officer was enjoying his audience. "Two weeks ago we had considerable excitement. They hanged a Negro out on the square for assaulting a white lady. I guess everything will be all right from now on."

I began to wonder what kind of place I was getting into but before I could continue the conversation, the whistle blew and the railroad coach leaned on the curve around a hill. Through the grimy windows, I could see the spires of Cumberland University—where Lebanon Law School was located. My dream was becoming reality. When I walked out of those doors beyond the oak-studded bluegrass campus, I would be able to swing my shingle proudly over a book-lined law office.

The college dray was at the depot platform, and already students from the incoming train were piling on it. I pitched my telescope bag and tiny trunk between the seats and piled aboard. Thirty minutes later I was shaking hands with my three roommates, R. Bradley Fentress from Murfreesboro, Tennessee (we later named our second son after him), B. Guy Smith from Montgomery, Alabama, and Casey Purnell from New York City—all sonorous, legal-sounding names. I started to say, "J. Searcy Bracewell, Sand Hill, Texas," but gave it up in favor of simply, "Searcy Bracewell, Sand Hill, Texas." The first hurdle was cleared without scratching a leg. I liked my roommates, and I liked what I saw of Lebanon Law School.

The law school was almost entirely disassociated from the rest of the university. Its building was about ten blocks from the campus of the academic school, but the students were allowed dormitory privileges on the main campus. The student body was about evenly divided between the students of law and those of the fine arts with about 150 in each division.

Monday morning, I matriculated into the law school, paying $150 for the semester tuition. I noticed as I mingled with the others that there seemed to be no cohesion or group interest among the law students. About equal numbers were from Tennessee and Texas; together, these states accounted for roughly 50 percent of the student body. The others were from all corners of the United States.

Carruthers Hall, the law school building, was an old two-story structure of red brick. It had two large classrooms separated by a wide hall, and across the back and opening into the hall was a sizable law library. Upstairs was an assembly room which would accommodate 300. It was dingy and showed frequent use by those from the tobacco-growing states. The first time I saw it, I commented to a fellow student, "If those lawyers-to-be miss legal points as often as they miss the spittoons, a lot of bandits will get themselves hung."

Three elderly men comprised the entire faculty: Judge Nathan Green, who was 88 years old and had taught in the school 60 years; Dr. Andrew B. Martin, 75, in his 30th year at Lebanon; and Judge E. E. Beard, a former justice of the Supreme Court who was still practicing law in Lebanon and devoting his evenings to conducting moot court for the fledgling attorneys.

Contrary to the practice of modern law schools, Lebanon taught only the textbooks from the recognized masters of the profession. No cases were used, and there were no case books in the library. There was, prominently placed, a collection of the reports of the Supreme Court of Tennessee. Dr. Martin had written a law book, *The History of the Lawsuit*, which was, in fact, an introduction to the study of law. *Parson on Contracts, Cooley on Torts, Greenleaf on Evidence, Kent on Real Property, Storey on Equity in Jurisprudence,* and *Stephens on Pleadings* were only a few of the texts taught. These books are to law what Shakespeare, Milton, and Bacon are to English literature.

The method of instruction was unique, though amazingly simple. One hundred pages of "living" law was assigned for reading every day for six days each week—one book at a time. For Dr. Martin's classes, the quiz on the previous day's assignment began promptly at 9:00 in the morning and lasted for one hour and a half. For Judge Green's, the interrogation began at 10:30 a.m.

Through the years, these instructors had accumulated a

list of searching questions covering the entire subject matter of the lesson assigned. First, the teachers asked the questions and then from a list of class members called on someone to answer. In this way every member of the class was put at attention and had to be certain that he understood the query, or he would miss the opportunity to answer. There was no asking for a repetition or explanation of the question. The minute any student did so, the entire class began to stamp feet, and the inattentive or obtuse student was drowned out.

At first I resented this relentless regime, but I soon saw that if any student were permitted to ask questions or make a speech, the effectiveness of the class period would be destroyed. The professor had to step briskly to cover that 100 pages of "live, living law" during the hour and a half quiz. Since everyone was primarily interested in getting a law license in ten months, it all worked into a good system of instruction with the maximum knowledge obtained in the least possible time.

And so, for one long year, I managed to read 100 pages of 'live, living law' every day and—in addition—write a letter to Lola Blount every two weeks. Lola usually had something to write about in her letters, as she was writing from where I knew the people and the surroundings, but I had very little to say since I dared not write the thoughts with which I was most preoccupied. We inched along a little further and further until the year at last had passed without any fateful words or commitments having been made on paper. But it is only fair to say that a perfect understanding had been reached. Her family and immediate friends probably understood the undisclosed commitment as well as we did.

Each student at Lebanon Law School was required to participate in two moot court trials every semester. This gave him a minimum of four such trials during his stay at college. Four students took part in each trial, two to the side. Judge Beard, who presided and directed the mock legal contest, would assign the facts of the case to be tried. These were always sketchy. It was left up to the students to develop their own facts and prepare the case for trial. It was always surprising how the facts of one side seemed to dovetail into those of the other so that the fledgling lawyers were put on their mettle. In one sense, these were real trials.

For example, the assignment might be simply: "W. J. Brown sues Harold Smith on a note for $200 given as the purchase price for a span of mules. Smith defends on the ground that Brown practiced a fraud on him in representing that the mules were good work animals, but they turned out to be balky and at times would refuse—adamantly—to pull. The Plaintiff will be represented by Fentress and Purnell, and the Defendant by Guy Smith and Paul Bedford."

The court, as organized, was presided over by Judge Beard and had a clerk and a bailiff, like a regular legal contest. It devolved upon the students representing the plaintiff to draw the complaint or petition. The sheriff (a student) would serve the citation on the defendant and make his return to the court, showing such service. It was then the duty of the students representing the defendant to file their answer and join issue.

On the day of trial, a jury of three was selected, and the case proceeded just as in a court of record with all its formalities and dignity. Two or three witnesses would be introduced, and each side would examine and cross-examine them and make its argument to the jury. All this was of inestimable value to the student, especially since the trial was presided over by a judge of such wide experience.

Some of the students from different states organized their own courts, which were presided over by some member of their club. This was designed to give them some familiarity with any peculiar phases of the practice in their own future spheres of work.

Another important phase of the well-rounded education at Lebanon Law School was debating. There were two debating societies, the Lex and Philomatheium. Any student was eligible to join—he simply enrolled in the society of his choice. No dues were required, and there were no expenses connected with this activity. No speakers were assigned to argue the question as it was altogether extemporaneous. The president would usually assign a lead-off man to state the question and take one side or the other. Subjects to be discussed on the succeeding night were posted on the bulletin board. Promptly at 7:30 p.m., the debate would begin. Usually there were only six or eight students present when the arguments started, but as the evening wore on and students drifted back from the town square where they had played pool or whiled away some time at the drug or book store, the crowd grew. Before the debate closed, some 25 or 30 students would be wanting to argue one point or another.

It would be difficult to think of any system that could provide a better vehicle for developing extemporaneous speaking and argument—as well as self-control. Sometimes the debate got pretty hot. Since I enrolled at Lebanon before the United States entered World War I and a good many of the students were sympathetic with the Germans, the usually-assigned questions were drawn from the reported conduct of the war. This not only furnished incentive to enter debate, but was incendiary.

"We brought the war to our own shores," I recalled later, with my eyes twinkling in remembrance.

The university itself had a football team of sorts, though not many students paid attention to it. Neither did opposing teams. The most one-sided football game on record may be the one in which Georgia Tech beat Cumberland University 216-0.

The atmosphere of the university—and the town in general— was that of the Old South. Judge Green might have been "Mr. Confederacy" himself. His home was just one block from the law building, and every morning he could be seen walking toward his classroom with a measured tread, cane in hand, wearing a frock-tail coat and black bow tie, his classic face garnished by an aggressive goatee. Judge Beard, too, was the soul of dignity. Dr. Martin dressed and acted more informally.

The most-renowned student who ever attended the law school was Joseph Weldon Bailey, afterwards United States Senator from Texas. He was acclaimed as one of the greatest orators alive. His fiery forensic delivery was built around the heroism of the Old South. He frequently went out to the foot of the monument in the public square, threw his hat on the ground and roared his approval of the Confederacy. Since nearly half the men living at that time had participated in the

War between the States, Bailey soon was surrounded by several hundred listeners, many of whom boosted him for any election in which he was candidate.

This tiny law school produced such men as Secretary of State Cordell Hull, Justice Lamar of the United States Supreme Court, Chief Justice Gaines of the Supreme Court of Texas, Blair of Missouri, Holloway of Oklahoma, Collins of Florida, and Wright Patman of Texas. There is an ever-longer roll of lawyers who have distinguished themselves in private practice.

If the history of law schools in America is ever written, there will probably be an unanswered question as to why this old law school in the hills of Tennessee was so successful.

I could answer that question decades after my graduation. First of all, it was the one-year course, which has now been abandoned everywhere. That drew to the school children of adversity but of great potential, who were determined to succeed and who would have had little chance otherwise. Next, I would put the teaching of old texts rather than the casebook system. After spending 45 years in the active practice of law, I find that when the most difficult questions arise, more light will be shed upon them by the old text writers than from the latest cases in the current reports. Finally, the three old men—Judge Green, Judge Beard, and Dr. Martin, guiding lights of the school—helped to shape the character of the students who were to enter the battles of life, as well as law. I say this, I might add, with no thought of discrediting the eminent lawyers who succeeded them.

Graduation! With trembling hand, I received my diploma from the hands of Judge Green. I stopped off in Texarkana to take the Texas bar examination—which was some ordeal itself—at the Court of Civil Appeals in Texarkana on my way home. About 40 boys from Texas took the examination, and only one failed.

Once the bar examination was behind me, Lola met me at the train late one Saturday afternoon, unashamed and dressed in a white dress, blue shoes, and a broad-brimmed straw hat and carrying a fancy silk umbrella. I was serious enough to remember these little details. I felt a little seedy, but I was beaming with delight. We strolled leisurely over the hill to her home about a mile away. Mr. and Mrs. Blount and Alma received me quite graciously. After it was all over, I probably felt a lot like a doughboy emerging safely from a foxhole after a hard day's fighting.

I stayed until late in the night—10:30 p.m. was late in those days. What had become well understood by intimation and inferred from correspondence became finalized and formalized that evening. It might have seemed to some an anticlimax to a curious courtship, but we were at least quite happy and well satisfied.

Two months later, on June 23, 1915, I received my license to practice law in the State of Texas. It was just six years after my graduation from Bedias—six long, hard years, however.

There was no way for me to know that another six years, in some ways more difficult, would elapse before I could claim to be a reasonably competent and self-sustaining lawyer.

Life After Law School

LOLA KNEW—as well as I—that I was dead broke. After I had taken the oath of office as a lawyer before my father's lifelong friend, W. S. Stapley of Bedias, the big question confronting me was what to do next. Although I was flat broke, I felt sure it would be a big mistake to do any more teaching. Since I was now a duly-licensed lawyer, I was ready to begin the "starvation" which I had heard so much about. I had to decide whether I should locate in a small town in Grimes or one of the adjoining counties or go to the city. I had many kinfolks and acquaintances in Grimes County and also in Walker and Madison counties. I knew absolutely no one, whatsoever, in any of the cities. But by talking to lawyers of mature experience who were friendly, I learned that the best of them were hardly making a living in the surrounding towns. The war in Europe had settled down to a stalemate, and economic conditions here were very much depressed.

With these considerations against settling in the small towns, I decided to settle in a city. Houston—being only 75 miles away—suggested itself as the most likely place to get a start. At that time, it had a population of 138,000. I had been there only once before, and most of the information which I had about it was gathered from the newspapers. Much of the publicity was centered around the development of navigation on the Houston Ship Channel, which had only recently been opened—and on the Rice Hotel, which had just opened and was considered the leading hotel in the Southwest. William Marsh Rice had died and left his immense fortune toward the establishment of a great university in Houston and his murderer, Albert T. Patrick, had been tried and convicted in New York. There was much publicity about the case and estate—which he had left for the university—and about the contest of a will through which Patrick had contrived to get most of Rice's property for himself. I thought there must be quite a few other young lawyers in Houston going through the starvation period and decided that I had as well go there where I would at least have others sharing my situation. So, I finally made the decision, determined not to look back until I had established myself.

The economy of the country was then in terrible condition, since cotton was selling at five cents per pound. The best lawyers in that whole area were not making operating expenses. Even if I had not passed the bar examination, it would be useless to settle anywhere around Roans Prairie. Houston was being publicized as a rapidly-growing city, and we decided that I had as well take a chance there as anywhere else for the inevitable starvation period. We tentatively set the wedding one year away. Neither of us at that time realized just how real and intense this starvation period would be.

◆◆◆

Move to Houston and Harrisburg

I ARRIVED IN Houston with less than $25 in my pocket and luckily found a friend with whom I took lodging—at a more or less nominal sum—in a cheap rooming house out on Caroline Street. We could get our meals at old Colby's Restaurant for 25 cents each, and I thought that I could subsist very well until I could find someplace to get a toehold in the practice of law. Like nearly every other young lawyer, I had an ambition to get with a large firm that had considerable business and work for a salary for a period, gradually moving up into a participation in the firm. There were several sizable firms at that time, such as Baker, Botts, Parker & Garwood; Andrews, Ball & Streetman; and Lane, Wolters & Storey. I made the rounds of each of them and soon reached the conclusion that they were about as hard-pressed as the lawyers in the country. While a few young lawyers with pull were getting on with the larger firms, they were hired at a salary of $50 per month. I tried this for about 30 days, and my resources were completely exhausted.

A friend suggested that I go to the YMCA and talk to the secretary, who might suggest something that would enable me to survive. He suggested that I try to get office space with a lawyer by the name of A. E. Dawes who lived at the YMCA and had an office in the Stewart Building. Maybe I could get enough business to support myself and maybe help him in some of his work. Dawes was a good man with high ideals, but had absolutely no business whatsoever. He gave me a desk in his office, and I got my printer brother, Ernest, to stake me to some letterhead and envelopes. I boldly proclaimed to the world that I was a lawyer ready for business!

But no business came. Lawyers were fighting for every little case that had a few dollars in it. Finally, someone recommended me to a Negro burglar who had 50-odd charges against him. He had three or four pistols and a couple of watches. Somehow it did not occur to me that they were probably stolen. He sold them all for $15 and paid me that to represent him—with, of course, a promise to pay substantially more if, as, and when I got him acquitted.

The district attorney's staff was very ably manned by John H. Crooker, the D.A., and by Tom Branch, Tom Harris, Frank Williford, and Ewing Boyd. The cases came up for trial within a few days after I was employed, and my client got more than 50 years in the penitentiary. This was most discouraging, and I began to see that there was no honorable way of sustaining myself in the practice of law unless I could get something with a little salary attached to it.

One day while in the coffee shop, I sat down next to a man and introduced myself to him. I learned that he was Joe Lyle, the county school superintendent. He was quite sympathetic and congenial, since I could speak his language pertaining to school problems. I told him frankly that I was having a pretty rough go trying to get started practicing law.

In about another week I chanced to meet Professor Lyle in the coffee shop again, and he asked me if I would be interested in taking a job at Harrisburg teaching mathematics. The high school mathematics teacher had just resigned on account of his health, and they were very anxious to get somebody to fill the place immediately. He told me the job paid $70 per month, but he thought there would be a pretty fair opportunity for advancement. I told him that I was definitely interested and would let him know shortly.

I conferred with a distinguished lawyer of many years' experience, Captain J. V. Lea, who was virtually retired. He told me to by all means take the position, because it would not only enable me to sustain myself but also introduce me to many of the parents of the pupils. In that way, I could build up my acquaintance that would enable me to get started practicing law. He stated further than many of the boys and girls whom I taught would, within a few years, become men and women of affairs in Houston and would be a source of much legal business. In later years, I found that he was absolutely correct. Captain Lea agreed to vouch for my credit at Zindler's for a new suit of clothes. I went back to the superintendent and told him that I would take the teaching job. I immediately wound up my meager affairs with Dawes and my rooming house and took the streetcar toward Harrisburg. While the streetcar did not extend that far, Harrisburg was only about a mile from the terminus, and I could very easily walk the balance of the distance.

Harrisburg was about eight miles from downtown Houston. I knew something of its historical background. It had been the home of many revolutionary patriots during the Texas War of Independence, and it was the second capital of Texas. Also, it was settled before Houston and for a long time was the leading city in that area. It was the head of navigation on Buffalo Bayou and a short distance from where Deaf Smith captured Santa Ana. It was the terminus of the first railroad that was ever constructed in Texas, and the railroad roundhouse and shops still were located there. And it was the center of wealth and culture during, and immediately preceding, the Civil War.

Due to the shortsightedness of some of Harrisburg's wealthiest citizens, who held their property for fabulous prices—and to a general local lack of enterprising spirit—the Allen Brothers had gone further up the bayou and laid out the townsite of Houston. Within a few years, Houston had outstripped Harrisburg and not only had taken the industries, but the railroad roundhouses and machine shops as well. Harrisburg had fallen into decay. At the time I went there to teach school, it was a desolate and dismal looking ghost town. It was still pretty much under the influence and direction of the surviving pioneer citizens, such as Judge John G. Tod, C. H. Milby, Gus Shepherd, Jim Deady, and Tobe Collins.

Magnolia Park, on the eastern side of Houston, had been sectioned off into building lots, and the streetcar extended there to Brays Bayou on the north. I got off the streetcar to find an old rickety bridge across the bayou. Leading up the hill was a shell road, the only street in the commercial area. The shell had been ground into a fine dust, and I literally waded through it to the school. There were no sidewalks, and the little business houses such as grocery stores, barber shops, saloons, and pool halls were on either side of the street. There were some six or eight saloons in the town, and that seemed to be the principal industry.

After getting a boarding house and being installed as a teacher, I soon met all of the faculty and the board of trustees of the school—all of whom became my staunch friends and in later life, my clients. Since I was a fairly good mathematician, the teaching assignment was not too difficult, and I had much time to mix with the people. Among the topics of conversation was how the old nesters had blocked the growth of Harrisburg and gobbled up the land and let Houston become a great metropolitan city—while their own town had fallen into decay.

One day there was a great flurry of excitement because it was reported that on the day before, the City of Houston's City Council—acting under its annexation powers—had swooped down and incorporated into the boundaries of Houston all of the valuable land along the ship channel. In fact, it had taken into Houston a part of Harrisburg, including the residence of Judge John G. Tod, but had left out most of his land holdings. It was apparent that if Houston could get a part of Harrisburg one day, it could come back any day following and get the balance of it. Then the entire area would be subjected to Houston taxes, possibly with very little hope of benefit. Houston officials gave as their excuse that it was necessary to control the property adjacent to the Houston Ship Channel for the purposes of policing the channel and protecting the development of navigation.

A public indignation meeting was called at the school building. For a large city like Houston to reach out and gobble up an adjacent area for no reason—other than that it contained valuable tax properties—and to do so without any notice of any kind or character to the people involved—and without giving them a right to be heard—was an outrage which was unthinkable. I was, of course, called on to have my say, and I was sure that the law provided a remedy for a people who had been so wronged. But after everybody had relieved their pent-up feelings about the matter, the question resolved itself into one of what to do about it.

Judge Tod had a distinguished career as a district judge and was too experienced not to know that there was nothing that could be done about what the city had already accomplished. He did suggest that a city the size of Houston could not annex an incorporated town, and we could at least save what was left by immediately incorporating the balance of Harrisburg. There were two methods of incorporation available, one of which had a tax-levying limit of 25 cents and the other a limit of $1.50. Naturally, the pioneer landowners in control selected the type with the 25-cent limit.

Judge Tod prepared all of the incorporation papers. The proceedings were inaugurated. The county judge called the election for about 30 days off, at the end of which period the citizens of Harrisburg voted unanimously to incorporate. Then, within about a month following, it was necessary to have another election to choose the officials, consisting of a board of five aldermen, a mayor, and a city marshal. The whole thing soon blossomed into a red-hot political campaign. Gus Shepherd was the candidate for mayor representing the pioneer or conservative element and James S. Deady was the candidate representing the younger and liberal element.

Deady had wide experience in politics. He had been justice of the peace of the area and also chairman of the Harris County Board of Education. It was a close vote, but Deady won and served the city in that capacity for 12 years. While not too active, I had aligned myself with the Deady faction. After the election, I spent a weekend at Bedias. When the council met that Saturday night, it created the office of city attorney and unanimously elected me. It was probably more of a joke than it was meant to be serious because they dispatched a telegram to me at Bedias notifying me of my election. With Bedias being just a small community where everybody knows everything that goes on, the news soon spread all over town that I had been elected City Attorney of Harrisburg. Although I suffered no illusions as to the importance of the job, still it served to give me a little prestige and standing as a lawyer, not only in Harrisburg, but in Bedias as well.

After incorporation, the demand immediately arose to get such improvements as water, sewers, sidewalks, and hard-top streets, because it was only a question of time until Houston would, through some devious method, incorporate the whole area into its spreading boundaries. As city attorney, I was called on to evolve some method whereby the tax rate might be increased and bonds issued to obtain these improvements. Although I had represented petty offenders in speeding and crap-shooting cases, this job of enlarging the powers of the city was the first real legal problem I had been called on to solve. I found that the law did provide a way that it could be done without an election by the people, and within a short time the city government had been converted into that type which would authorize a rate of $1.50 and had the power to issue the bonds for improvements.

My term as a teacher of mathematics at the Harrisburg School resulted in a degree of satisfaction to the patrons—and having gained the favor of the school board and the principal, the second year I was transferred to the principalship of the Magnolia Park School in the same district. This school had 11 teachers and paid $100 per month. Lola Blount and I had kept up a kind of guerilla courtship during all of this time, and the lucrative salary of $100 per month as principal of the Magnolia Park Elementary School made me think seriously of matrimony.

Anyway, we decided on a "for better or worse" adventure and set the date. We were married at the Blount home in Roans Prairie on the 24th of December, 1916.

I was just about square with the world. I had two jobs, one as principal of the Magnolia Park School and the other as the non-paying job of City Attorney of the City of Harrisburg, so we did not delude ourselves into the belief that the starvation period was over.

We secured a little furnished cottage in Harrisburg, and I began to do a little legal work on the side. Having these additional responsibilities, the school board at Harrisburg decided to raise my salary to $125 for the second year as principal—my third year with the school system—and the city began to issue its bonds for public improvements. I had to work hard as city attorney to get up and market each of these bond issues, so the city adopted the policy of paying me one percent of the issue as compensation. The first was for $50,000, resulting in a fee of $500, and within about a year they had another issue of $200,000, resulting in a fee of $2,000. I was also engaged to incorporate two or three companies to participate in the rapidly-growing economy, all of which proved invaluable to me later.

Now, while Lola fully shared my exultation in all of this, neither of us realized that our hardship had, by no means, ended. Being deprived of going to college was not an unmixed evil, and the skills which Lola had acquired at home during the time she would have been at school began to show up to great advantage now. Lola had learned to cook, to buy groceries, to sew, to decorate a home, to plant and develop a garden, to can fruits and vegetables, and, above all, to be an ideal hostess—after the manner and excellence of her mother. Early in our married life, she won a citywide cooking contest.

My friends there had been on the winning side of the different political campaigns, notably those for county judge and district attorney. I was startled to be informed by one of them that one of the assistant district attorneys in charge of tax suits had resigned and there was a possibility of my getting the job. The district attorney and the county judge had to agree upon the assistant, and it so happened that I was about the only one they could agree on, since all of my gang in the East End had supported both candidates. So I found myself at the end of 1918 an assistant district attorney of Harris County, although in a very minor position. The job paid $150 per month.

This, of course, terminated my work in the teaching profession. I found myself at last a very busy lawyer representing the City of Harrisburg and also serving as assistant district attorney in charge of tax matters for the county. Although the pay was not much, it enabled us to get along. And we did so for a period of two years, when I felt that unless I got out and established myself in an independent law practice, I would just be a salaried official from there on out. This feeling led to my resignation as assistant district attorney. I continued on as City Attorney for Harrisburg.

Although the salary in the district attorney's office was only $150 per month, I had saved up some of the money which came to me for handling the bond issues for the City of Harrisburg. I also had a lucky break in buying and selling some secondhand lumber in cooperation with two Harrisburg friends; that venture netted me $1,000. Lola and I had bought a home in Harrisburg at a quite reasonable price, and after squaring up everything, I had on hand approximately $2,000. Since I was leaving the district attorney's office and going into practice for myself, it occurred to me that this was about the last time that Lola and I would have time in which to take a vacation. Searcy, Jr. had been born in the meantime and was now two years old. Also, I was impressed with the fact that the world was undergoing a profound change. The war had ended, and Woodrow Wilson was making a strenuous effort to get the League of Nations established.

Columbia University

I BECAME VERY much obsessed with the idea that the League of Nations presaged a new world order, and I was anxious to become a part of it. John Bassett Moore had been widely publicized as one of the architects of the League of Nations, and he was a professor of law at Columbia University. It occurred to me that I might go up to Columbia and get tied up with something that would allow me to participate in some way in the League of Nations. The Republican Party had turned its back on Wilson and all of his programs and nominated Senator Harding for the presidency. Harding was the soul of reaction, and he made an issue out of the League of Nations. The Democrats nominated Governor Cox of Ohio, and he became a very dedicated advocate of Wilson's program. It all appealed to me so much that Lola and I decided we would take a break in my activities in Houston and go to New York for three months. There I would attend John Bassett Moore's lectures at Columbia University and at the same time participate in the political campaign. She, of course, would have a full-time job taking care of our two year old.

It all worked well except that Cox was badly beaten by Harding, and the League of Nations received its death blow. However, I registered with the speakers' bureau of the

Democratic National Committee and was sent to a good many places to speak in New York. It gave me wonderful experience as a political speaker. Moore was not the dynamic personality that I had anticipated. Although I attended his lectures, after the election of Harding I virtually lost interest in the possibilities of the League of Nations. Harlan F. Stone, afterwards Chief Justice of the United States Supreme Court, was dean of the law school. His lectures were extremely helpful and became treasured memories.

Lola and I saw many things of interest. It is said that a person can stay in New York an entire year and go to a different place of interest every day. We found it so, and although the trip did not amount to too much in a professional way, it was all helpful to us later in life. The fact that I had been to Columbia University added somewhat to my prestige as a lawyer.

◆◆◆

Our Return Home

WE RETURNED FROM New York to Houston by boat, landing in Galveston about January 1, 1920. The newspapers from Houston gave almost daily accounts of the rise of the Ku Klux Klan in the South—and particularly in Houston and Harris County. The organization professed a code of lofty principles, but it went further than that and undertook to correct the morals of the people by channels other than through the courts of law. There were several instances of people of supposed bad character being beaten and driven out of communities—the most shocking was that of a woman in Teneha in East Texas. I became more and more concerned, and since the district attorney of the county appeared to be so weak in his prosecutions as to connive at the activities of the Klan, I decided to run for district attorney and make the enforcement of the law against the Ku Klux Klan a principal issue.

I became associated with the office of Cooper & Merrill,

two very able lawyers and began to attract enough business to sustain us. If I could only be elected district attorney, I could receive a good salary and engage in a fight that was very much to my liking. In short, I would have it made.

It all went to show how much I had to learn in politics. I had gone on the theory all the time that enough people would stand up and fight for principles to prevail in almost any political campaign. The district attorney took a middle-of-the-road course, and the Klan candidate was somewhat open and frank in his advocacy of the Klan and all of its operations. The middle-of-the-roader began to equivocate, and for a while it looked like the great body of people who were opposed to the Klan would support my candidacy. But the old cry started, "He is young and can't win," and the other man was said to be a lot stronger against the Klan than his public statements would indicate. In the end, he got the great bulk of the anti-Klan vote, and the Klansman was elected in a walk. He beat both of us by a large majority. This election was in the summer of 1922—the Democratic primary—but in those days equivalent to election because the Republican party didn't bother to nominate a candidate.

Chapter 3

The Ferguson Campaign [1]

J. S. Bracewell's defeat in the district attorney's race only crystallized his determination to fight the growing menace of the Ku Klux Klan with every weapon at his command. Clandestine mob violence had been the order of the day. If the Klan could so control a political election that its favored candidate could win, it was time some means were found to stop its machinations.

Strangely, that means took the form of a woman—Miriam A. (whose initials spelled "Ma") Ferguson, wife of a former governor who had been removed from office by impeachment. The power behind her was her impeached husband, ex-governor James E. Ferguson. Chairman of the Harris County forces for the election of Ma Ferguson was J. S. Bracewell.

However, several years of background to this development need to be told.

Young lawyer Bracewell had been following the career of "Farmer Jim" Ferguson since 1914. Prior to that year, James E. Ferguson—who operated a country bank in Temple—had scarcely been heard of outside Bell County.

Three years earlier, while Bracewell was attending Sam Houston State Teachers' College in Huntsville, the state of Texas experienced a very bitter political campaign for the prohibition of the sale of intoxicating liquors. The Prohibition

[1] As told to Rev. Harold Dye through personal visits and correspondence with J.S. Bracewell.

Party was led by Col. Thomas H. Ball of Houston, a former Huntsville resident.

Although it had been widely predicted that the prohibitionists did not have a chance, the returns showed a surprising prohibition sentiment. In fact, they led the election returns until the heavily Mexican precincts in the Rio Grande Valley came in and put the Wets in the lead by about 8,000 votes. The great majority of Texans believed that these Southwest Texas returns were fraudulent and that the Pros had really won. They immediately began a hue and cry to resubmit the question at the first convenient statewide election.

Texas did not have a runoff primary at that time, so the high man of those running would be declared the party's nominee. Since there was virtually no Republican party in Texas at that time, the Democratic nomination was tantamount to election. Many politicians who had actively participated on both sides of the prohibition campaign were very eager to be governor. Among these was Col. Ball. In addition to him, the prohibitionists had such leaders as Cone Johnson and Cullen Thomas. An equal number of leaders in the "Wet" camp were eager to head the state. Among these were Col. Jake Walters, who had led the anti-prohibition campaign, and W. A. Hanger and Louis Worsham.

Since they were all prominent men, even the wisest political prognosticator could not possibly make an intelligent guess as to who would likely be elected governor. Each side began to devise means of selecting one outstanding Pro and one outstanding Anti to lead their respective factions. There was much publicity about the plan.

Banker James Ferguson had not taken any part whatsoever in the prohibition campaign. All at once, like a bolt out of the blue, he announced that he was going to be a candidate for governor. He said he didn't give a tinker's damn who the Pros got together on, or who the Antis got together on, because they were all merely a bunch of politicians entirely out of sympathy with the common man. He declared himself in favor of burying the issue of prohibition and getting on with some real bread and butter issues. He also announced that if he were elected governor, he was going to put a stop to all of the prohibition agitation and that if any legislation on the matter were passed, it would get his veto "where the chicken got the axe."

He further said that the tenant farmers of Texas, who made up about 41 percent of the population at that time, were not getting a square deal. Under the age old pioneer plan, the tenant went out and rented a place and if he had his own teams and equipment, he paid ⅓ of the corn and ¼ of the cotton as rental. But since the pioneer days, the old system had been perverted. Landlords were now charging a cash bonus in addition to percentages of the crops. Ferguson proposed to pass a law which would rigidly limit the rentals to ¼ of the cotton and ⅓ of the corn. That was his main plank.

All of the wise boys laughed at Ferguson's announcement. They figured that he could not possibly influence the main contest between the Pros and the Antis. However, they soon began to take a second look at him. Ferguson was a tall, brunette man. Although he was not too eloquent that early in his career, he knew how to speak the language of the common man and tip the mask off political hypocrisy.

The brewers and the distillers in Texas then began to reason among themselves a little. Of course they wanted a stop to the prohibition agitation, and they didn't give a hoot what became of the Antis. They found out that Ferguson had been a lifelong Anti. Since he wanted to leave matters pertaining to prohibition right where they were, it dawned on them that their interests coincided. And, of course, these businessmen were the ones who were going to put up the money in the election.

The caucus of the "Pros" (prohibitionists) at Dallas went through on schedule and was well attended. After a lot of speech making and hurrahing, they nominated Col. Thomas H. Ball as their candidate for governor.

The Antis had their convention a few days later. To every-body's amazement, only a handful attended. They held their caucuses in hotel lobbies. Since the politicians could not stir up any enthusiasm to back their candidates, the Antis adjourned without nominating anybody. It soon became apparent that they would have a two-candidate race all right, but those two candidates would be Col. Ball and Jim Ferguson. Col. Ball was a former congressman, a member of one of the leading corporate law firms of Texas, and a man who was known in every hamlet and village in the state since he had led the prohibition forces. While he was not too old, he looked like a patriarch with his iron gray mustache and long, flowing locks. It seemed as if it would be a one-sided contest. Col. Ball announced his platform first. Much of it was devoted to prohibition, advocating its resubmission to the people.

Ferguson opened his campaign in a small crossroads village in North Texas, where tenant farmers abounded. He tore into the colonel like a wild bore. He dubbed Ball's platform "just like an old Mother Hubbard dress, in that it covered everything and touched nothing." He excoriated Col. Ball as being the candidate of the railroads, which Ball's firm represented, and a big politician who had gotten together with the big boys at Dallas to run the state. During the campaign, Ferguson revealed that Col. Ball was a member of the fashionable Houston Club, where liquor was sold and served and the big boys whiled away their leisure hours playing poker.

All of this was true, but of course, not so bad in itself had the Colonel not projected himself as a leader of the Lily Whites. The whole thing made him appear to be a genuine hypocrite.

The people in Huntsville naturally took a great interest in the campaign of their native son, and J. S. Bracewell participated in it to the extent of his ability on the side of Col. Ball. He made two or three speeches for him, but the campaign was pitched in such a manner that it was utterly impossible to win, and Ferguson swept the state.

Although many people considered Ferguson a demagogue after he took the oath of office, he immediately began to display rare executive talents. He called on the leaders of the state to develop a legislative program and gained the confidence of both prohibitionists and anti-prohibitionists. It was not many months before he was widely regarded as having extraordinary ability to lead the state.

However, it was also not long before his policies began to stir up much opposition, primarily because he was anxious to develop the opportunities in country schools and rural areas, but somewhat at the expense of the University of Texas and other institutions of higher learning. Of course, many of the leaders of Texas finance, politics, and education were graduates of the University of Texas and very much devoted to it. When his first term was drawing to a close, they took a leaf out of Farmer Jim's book and ran a country blacksmith by the name of Williams against him. The campaign was quite spirited, but Ferguson was reelected by a big majority.

Ferguson was a man of unrelenting animosities, a trait which showed up pretty early in the legislative session following his reelection. When the appropriations bill was presented to him, he objected that it had incorporated entirely too much money for the university and stated that the legislature had gone hog wild over higher education. He strongly recommended that many of the juicy items be cut from the bill.

The legislature was unyielding, and sent the bill back to him with slight changes. While it was on his desk, a highly-organized band of demonstrators came down and surrounded the capitol—even throwing epithets at him through the windows of his executive office. Ferguson was so enraged that he vetoed the entire appropriations bill. Since the session was about over, nothing could be done about it during that session, and it was necessary to call a special session to make appropriations to run the state's institutions of higher learning.

The legislature met in an atmosphere of anger and determination. The university leaders were adamant for a liberal appropriation for the school, and Ferguson was just as strongly opposed. The House appointed a committee to draw up impeachment charges. After lengthy deliberation, they filed them—many in number. While the main issue was the university, the leaders saw that Ferguson could not be impeached on this alone. Some of his own crowd had gone over to the university's side and leaked to the committee that Ferguson had taken a lot of state money and put it in his own bank in Temple, contrary to Texas law. While there was no evidence that he had personally profited by doing this, it greatly inflamed the situation. In addition, one of the brewer representatives leaked the fact that Ferguson had accepted a large sum of money from the breweries to run his campaign for reelection.

Bracewell had been a staunch opponent of Ferguson, but he began to feel that enmity toward him had gone entirely too far. While Ferguson had done wrong, still his faults leaned to virtue's side in that all of his efforts were toward alleviating the condition of the underdog as opposed to the special interests of the state.

Though Bracewell had received his teacher's certificate and had taught three years, his interest grew in the political affairs developing in Texas, particularly the impeachment. W. L. Dean, the senior member of the firm where Bracewell studied law in Huntsville, was elected to the Texas Senate. He was quite an able lawyer and an outstanding leader of the prohibition element. When the Senate resolved itself into a high court to try Governor Ferguson on the impeachment charges, Senator Dean was elected presiding officer and conducted the trial.

Of course, this gave Bracewell an interest to side with Dean, although he had begun to sympathize with Governor Ferguson. After a long and bitter trial, Ferguson was impeached on several counts and driven from office. He gathered up his personal effects and left the capital in a storm of anger and bitterness.

Then began one of the longest political feuds that any state has ever experienced.

Ferguson was succeeded by Lt. Governor William P. Hobby. The next gubernatorial campaign started almost before Ferguson vacated the governor's mansion. There had been quite a lot of agitation for the ballot for women, and it was everywhere conceded that it would be necessary for a constitutional amendment to be passed permitting women to vote. However, the Texas Constitution had said nothing about voting in a *primary* election. So, after making the necessary appropriations for the university, the legislature took the precaution of passing an enactment permitting women to vote in all primary elections. There were few people in Texas who did not see at the time that the main motivation for the passage of the act was the theory that nearly all women were prohibitionists and would naturally feel grateful to the Hobby administration for having enfranchised them, thereby greatly helping Hobby's chances of election.

It was a furious campaign, but Ferguson could not stem the tide of the female vote. William P. Hobby was elected by a substantial majority. He served two years in addition to the unexpired Ferguson term and made a very creditable record. Both friends and enemies have now conceded that he was a very sincere man, devoid of all bitterness toward Ferguson. But Ferguson now had an issue that would not lie down. He had been unjustly kicked out of office and then forbidden his vindication by the people under the questionable mantle of women's suffrage. In defeat he still vowed to be vindicated by the people of Texas. That dogged determination was his chief claim to fame.

When Governor Hobby's term was over, the legislature further fortified itself against the return of Ferguson by providing that nobody could run for office in Texas who was not legally qualified to hold the office. (The impeachment rendered Ferguson ineligible.) The United States Senate campaign was coming up, and Ferguson and his friends discovered that the act of the legislature could not affect his qualification to run for the U. S. Senate. In the meantime, the legislature had passed another act providing that nobody could be nominated to public office in Texas unless he had received a clear majority of the vote, thereby necessitating a runoff election when a candidate did not receive a majority. This would vitally affect Ferguson's fortunes in the future.

And so Farmer Jim Ferguson began a campaign for the United States Senate. His principal opponent was Senator Earl B. Mayfield. His main issue was to vindicate himself and wipe out the disgrace that had been placed on him and his family by a very questionable impeachment. Senator Mayfield had been railroad commissioner and had built up quite a machine. After a stormy campaign, Mayfield succeeded in again thwarting Ferguson's ambition to get back in the saddle in Texas politics.

Fergusonism had been the cry in Texas for a decade, but on the horizon another political cloud had appeared that was to plague the state for many years—namely, the Ku Klux Klan. Senator Mayfield's election was in large part attributed to the active support of the Klan.

The next campaign was to be one for governor. Ferguson denounced the law disqualifying him from holding office and determined that he was going to run again and damned be he who tried to stop him. His opponents filed suit in the Supreme Court of Texas to enjoin the placing of his name on the ballot. The suit was successful. It looked like Ferguson was forever barred from holding a state office in Texas. Ferguson, of course, had developed great enmity toward the Klan because of its support of Mayfield.

When it was announced that Ferguson would not be permitted to run for governor, he promptly declared that he would have his wife's name put on the ticket in his place, and the people could vindicate him by electing Ma Ferguson. Farmer Jim began to denounce the activities of the Ku Klux Klan, but his main plea was for vindication of the great wrongs that had been done to him personally. His battle cry was "elect my wife and I'll bring in the wood and water."

The Klan never openly proclaimed its candidate, but it had a way of letting its support become known, and Judge Felix Robertson of Dallas was soon recognized as the candidate of the Klan. To everybody's amazement, and to the chagrin of quite a few, when the votes of the first primary were counted, Felix Robertson came in first, and Miriam A. Ferguson—whose only claim to fame up until that time had been that she was the meek, devoted wife of James E. Ferguson—came in second. She was, therefore, Judge Robertson's opponent because Robertson did not receive a majority of the vote—thereby necessitating a runoff. The Klan issue had at that time become so bitter that it overshadowed everything else.

J. S. Bracewell had run for district attorney during that same election and had taken a stand against the Klan. The Klan won so overwhelmingly in the D.A.'s race that there was not even a runoff. Since Ma Ferguson was now the anti-Klan candidate, Bracewell immediately cast his lot with the Fergusons, although he had never actively supported them before that time. The entire political landscape of the state was transformed. All over Texas, leading prohibitionists who had become hostile toward the Klan—and others who had become greatly embittered over the impeachment campaign—all joined forces behind Ma Ferguson. Bracewell made many speeches for Mrs. Ferguson. This threw him into the limelight, but probably ruined any chances he had for political preferment in Harris County. Ma Ferguson lost the county by a few hundred votes, but carried the state by a wide margin. Her victory was the beginning of the end of Ku Klux Klan domination in Texas.

During the campaign, Farmer Jim boasted that if the people would elect his wife governor, "they would get two governors for the price of one." It turned out very much that way. Mrs. Ferguson, while well educated, was totally domestically inclined and left the conduct of the office entirely to her husband. He handled all the patronage and conferred with the legislators and the leaders of Texas. It became a well-known fact that he was the power in Texas and that if anything came out of the governor's office, it had to be cleared with Farmer Jim. No one could see Ma until Farmer Jim "Pa" had okayed it!

But the hatreds built up in past controversies would not die down. Anti-Fergusonism soon overshadowed even the Klan. The forces against Ferguson nominated the brilliant young attorney general, Dan Moody, to run against Mrs. Ferguson for reelection. He defeated her and served two terms. Farmer Jim would not consider himself completely vindicated until Ma had been elected for a second term. When Moody had served his terms, his heir apparent was Ross Sterling, whom he had appointed chairman of the Highway Commission.

Sterling won, but he soon got into deep trouble. He was past president of the Humble Oil and Refining Company and owned banks and buildings. Trying to attend to his business and run the governor's office at the same time was too much for him. Miriam A. Ferguson came back for another try. The slogan of Farmer Jim's friends was "ME FOR MA." His opponents countered with "NO MA FOR ME—TOO MUCH PA." But this time Ma eked through with a small majority. During her second administration, Mrs. Ferguson developed into a very capable executive and had far more to do with the affairs of the state than she did in her first.

In later life, Bracewell said that he was wrong much of the time in his support of the Fergusons, but that his motives were of the highest. He respected Ferguson as the sincere friend of the underdog. He credited the stormy governor (who, in effect, served three terms in spite of impeachment) with being the one who broke the backbone of the politically-powerful Klan.

Bracewell might have gained some choice political spot for himself as the result of his strong support of the Fergusons, but he never held office under them, nor sought any reward. His interest then, as throughout his life, was in human rights.

J.S. Bracewell at Andrew Jackson's tomb at The Hermitage during law school. (Approximately 1915)

Graduation from Cumberland Law School, Lebanon, Tennessee. (1915)

J. S. BRACEWELL
CANDIDATE FOR
CRIMINAL DISTRICT ATTORNEY

I believe all classes are amenable to the law. ❧ I do not believe in permitting the worst criminals to turn state's evidence and escape punishment. I believe in every officer obeying the law. ❧ I favor the prosecution of any peace officer who administers the third degree. ❧ I am opposed to the Ku Klux Klan, or any other organization that pretends to be above the law. If elected I will enforce every law without fear, favor or discrimination, and if you believe in a government by law, and not by individuals, I want your support.

SUBJECT TO THE WILL OF THE PEOPLE, JULY 22nd, 1922

Campaign literature in race for District Attorney against the Ku Klux Klan. (July 22, 1922)

In his early law office in the Zindler Building. (1923)

"NEVER-AGAIN" SAYS TRAXLER BACK IN PEN

Recaptured Desperado, With Gunshot Wound, Arrives With Chain Around Neck.

Special to The Chronicle.

Huntsville, Aug. 14.—Roy (Pete) Traxler, 30, Texas bad man, arrived at the state prison shortly after noon Saturday, a month and four days after he escaped from Eastham farm with eight other desperadoes.

Traxler was returned from McAlester prison in Oklahoma, where he had been held in the hospital since he was wounded and recaptured by two Oklahomans whom he and a partner, Fred Tindol, had been holding as hostages.

When he arrived, in custody of Transfer Agent Bud Russell and his assistant, W. R. Crane, Traxler was dressed in a brown shirt and blue overall pants. He was chained by his neck to two other prisoners who had been picked up along the route. When queried as to how it felt to be back, Traxler replied:

"Well, it's a relief." He added that he had "had hell the whole time," while he was on escape, and also vigorously denied that his wife, now free on $10,000 bond after being charged with planting the weapons the convicts used in freeing themselves, had had anything to do with it.

"She had no more to do with it than you did," he said.

Pressed as to whether he "just got caught in a storm and joined the boys the day of the escape" or whether he had been in on the whole plot, he refused to reply. "I'd rather not comment on that," he said.

He also refused to reveal where he and Tindol had left Charlie Chapman, muchly wanted bank robber, who joined them in their flight.

When Warden W. W. Waid asked him how he felt, he replied that he thought he "would be able to make it, although I am pretty weak." He is recovering from a gunshot wound over the heart.

Warden Waid then gave instructions that he be taken to the hospital and be examined to determine whether he is able to be sent back to the prison farm where he escaped July 8.

Asked if he had any ideas regarding another flight, Pete smiled and said, "Never again."

He was serving life from Lipscomb County for robbery at the time he escaped. He was sentenced September 16, 1936.

Of the nine who escaped, two are dead. They are Fred Tindol and J. D. Reid, the waterboy who was killed the day of the break when he came into the open road and began firing at a posse of prison guards.

Two, Charlie Chapman, and Walter Belton, an illiterate Fort Worth habitual criminal, still are free.

W. B. A. Meeting.

The W. B. A. No. 58 Travel Club will meet at 1 p.m. Wednesday at the Milam Building. A regular business meeting will follow at 2 p.m.

Fentress and Searcy Bracewell.
(Approximately 1924)

During the Depression of the 30s, we kept a cow in the backyard.
(Pictured from left to right: Searcy Bracewell, our dog Jack, Bess
the cow, our father, and Fentress Bracewell.)

Joseph Searcy Bracewell standing in front of Broadway Baptist Church,
during construction (approximately 1936).

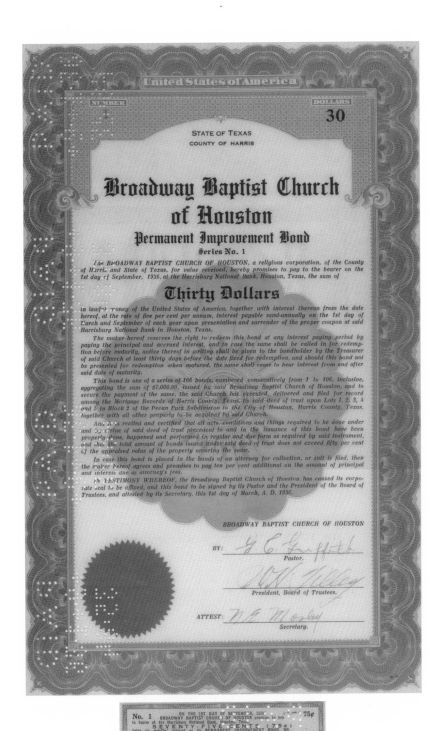

First bond issued by The Broadway Plan, March 1, 1936.

Monday, January 9, 1939

THE HOUSTON CHRONICLE
AND HERALD

PUBLISHED DAILY BY THE HOUSTON CHRONICLE PUBLISHING CO.
(REG. U. S. PATENT)   512-526 TRAVIS STREET, HOUSTON, TEXAS

JESSE H. JONES, President
G. W. COTTINGHAM, Editor
J. H. BUTLER, Business Manager
G. L. MIMS, Secretary and Treasurer

Entered July 25, 1902, at Houston, Texas, as Second-Class Matter Under Act of
Congress March 3, 1879.

MEMBER OF ASSOCIATED PRESS.

The Associated Press is exclusively entitled to the use for publication of all
news dispatches credited to it if not otherwise credited in this paper and also
the local news published herein.

WASHINGTON BUREAU.
B. N. TIMMONS, Correspondent, 1253-1255 National Press Bldg.

SUBSCRIPTION RATES.

Carrier Delivery or Mail in Texas	Outside Texas Mail, Payable in Advance
Daily and Sunday ....90c a month	Daily and Sunday.......$1.15 a month
Daily without Sunday.....65c a month	Daily without Sunday... 90c a month
Sunday only ....10c a copy	Sunday only ....10c a copy

The New Bar Association President

Able and vigorous leadership is assured the Houston Bar Association for the next 12 months with J. S. Bracewell as president.

His election without opposition and without any other name being mentioned for the office is indeed a high tribute to Jim Bracewell, and a well deserved one.

The forthright red-headed lawyer from Harrisburg does not mind fighting for what he thinks is right. As city attorney and school board president of Harrisburg, as president of the Harris County Taxpayers Association and as a member of the city charter commission, he demonstrated that time and again. Mr. Bracewell has held a number of positions of trust in this community and has established a reputation as a clear thinker and straight shooter.

Born on a farm near Bedias, in Grimes County, he received his early college education at Sam Houston State Teachers College, Huntsville. After teaching school six years—three in his native county and three in Harrisburg and Magnolia Park—he enrolled in Lebanon Law School of Tennessee. Upon graduation, he returned to practice law in Houston, and during the past 20 years has established himself as a leader in the legal profession of this city.

Our mother and dad engaged in a political mailout in 1957.

Our mother and father at The Farm in their early retirement (1960).

HOUSTON CHRONICLE

SECTION 2   HOUSTON, TEXAS, SUNDAY, JUNE 20, 1965   * * *   PAGE ONE

The Attorney Who Never Liked To Lose Looks Back on a Full Life

BY STAN REDDING
Chronicle Reporter

There are 20 names on the glass of the reception office of the law firm on the 18th floor of the First City National Bank Building.

The firm occupies an elegant suite of offices, with a decor as haughtily correct and as elegant as any Dior salon.

J. Searcy Bracewell Sr., whose name heads the list of lawyers, looked out the window toward Broadway and chuckled.

A Far Cry

"I hate to think of the rent the boys pay here," he said. "But it's a far cry from Harrisburg."

A far cry and 50 years, in fact, for this big man of gentle mien who is in his 73d year.

He came to Houston from Bedias in late 1914, a brand new law degree from Cumberland University law school (Lebanon, Tenn.) tucked under his arm.

He rented a back room in a Harrisburg drugstore for $15 a month and hung out his shingle.

His first client was a driver who had been arrested for exceeding the 20 m.p.h. speed limit.

Received $10

"He paid me $10," Bracewell recalls. "I lost the case in corporation court. I made the mistake of trying it before a jury. Folks were highly prejudiced against motor cars in those days.

"So I appealed it to county court, and won it there."

The case established a pattern. Bracewell made appeals his specialty and eventually

J. S. BRACEWELL SR.
Counts His Blessings

became one of the most successful appellate lawyers in the state. Bracewall admits he "didn't like to lose."

Two cases stand out in his memory. He defended Roy Traxler, an Oklahoman who became the nation's "Public Enemy No. 1" in the 1930s. Traxler, serving life at Eastham State Prison, escaped, disarming two guards in the process.

Lawmen hunted down the outlaw. The state sought the death penalty for Traxler who was indicted for armed robbery.

"I held that Roy—because of the cruelty then existing in the prisons—had to get out somehow, according to his method of thinking," said Bracewell.

"I argued that he took the guards' guns only on a temporary basis—that he did not intend to, and did not in fact, appropriate the weapons to his 'own use and benefit.'"

Won His Case

The judge so charged the jury, and the jury agreed with Bracewell. Roy was acquitted.

"Roy's now a respected, successful citizen back in Oklahoma," Bracewell said.

The second case was Miss Kate Scanlan's tiff with the light company during the depression. Bracewell in those days had offices in the Scanlan Building.

"Miss Kate believed the light company was charging too much for electricity, and she refused to pay," Bracewell said. "The light company said it was going to turn off the lights.

"She told me to file a suit. I knew we couldn't win, and I told her so, but she said to go ahead, so I did.

Lost All the Way

"I fought it all the way to the Supreme Court and lost it on every level.

"The light people were very sympathetic. They knew I officed there. They said they were sorry, but they'd have to cut off the lights.

"They did. And the minute they turned their lights off, Miss Kate turned her lights on.

"She'd spent all the time we consumed in litigation having a generator plant installed in the basement."

Miss Kate and the light company, Bracewell remembers, later settled their feud.

If Houston has served the man from Bedias well, he also

has given his time and talents to his community and his fellow man, in education, public service and religion.

He was principal of old Franklin School, president of the Harrisburg School Board, city attorney of Harrisburg, assistant district attorney of Harris County, president of the Harris County Taxpayers Assn., chairman of the Port Commission, and—until earlier this year—chairman of the natural resources division in the attorney general's office.

Bracewell is proudest of originating the "Broadway plan" of church finance, first used at Bracewell's Broadway Baptist Church, 7300 Bowie.

Bracewell, in 1936, proposed a simple plan for financing the expansion of churches and the building of new ones: Sell interest-bearing bonds based on the church's income.

To date, more than 400 churches have been aided or built under the plan, and more than $88 million in "Broadway plan" bonds have been issued across the nation.

Takes No Credit

Characteristically, Bracewell declines credit here, too.

"It was a divine pattern that followed us as we toiled," he said of the plan's inception and growth.

He and his wife of 50 years retired last year to Roans Prairie, where he now lives. But Atty. Gen. Waggoner Carr called him out of that retirement to work in the natural resources division of Carr's office.

He comes to Houston weekly now, drawn by his deep love of the law.

"But I'm going to quit for good," he says.

Fentress Bracewell and Searcy Bracewell—together with their mother, Lola Blount Bracewell—at The Farm (early 80s).

Appendix 1

A Few of J. S. Bracewell's Memorable Cases

A Death Sentence

"Your name is Andrew McDonald, and you reside at Bedias in this county of Grimes?"

"Yes, sir."

"Mr. McDonald, you have resided in this county practically all your life, have you not?"

"Yes, sir."

"And you are now and have been for some time the president of the White Man's Union of this county?"

"Yes, sir."

"The White Man's Union was organized in this county about 50 years ago, was it not?"

"Yes, sir."

"And the main purpose of its organization is to keep the Negroes from voting or holding office in this county, is it not?"

"Well, that might be partly it, but it also distributes the offices in the county. You see, Grimes County is a long county, and the largest town, Navasota, is located at one end. Before the organization of the Union, all the county officials usually came from Navasota, because they out-voted the rest of us. Under the White Man's Union, every precinct in the county has a representative in the county government. Every four years, the White Man's Union has a drawing for the different offices by precinct, with each precinct getting a county office."

"But, Mr. McDonald, isn't it true that the Union was organized primarily to keep the Negroes from participating in any politics?"

"Well, sir, that's mainly the truth."

"Is it not true, Mr. McDonald, that in your entire lifetime, not a single Negro has voted in this county?"

"Well, I don't believe I remember of one voting."

"Isn't it true that shortly prior to the organization of the White Man's Union, a combination of Negroes and Republicans had ruled the county ever since carpet-bag days?"

"Yes, sir, that is true."

"And didn't most of the voters combine themselves into the White Man's Union for the express purpose of keeping the Negroes from voting?"

"Well, yes. We didn't want them to vote. Of course, we couldn't control the general election, but the majority of the people in the county joined the White Man's Union. We have our own primary and, of course, the result has been that all government officials have belonged to the White Man's Union."

"Is it not true that no Negroes have been drawn on the juries in this county during your whole lifetime?"

"Well, no. There have been a few of them drawn."

"But isn't it true that you've never known of a Negro serving on a jury in any court in this county?"

"Yes, that's true. The lawyers always struck them off."

"Isn't it true, Mr. McDonald, that a Negro has never served on a grand jury in this county during your lifetime?

"Well, no, that's not true. We had heard that if you didn't have a Negro on the grand jury, it wouldn't be legal to indict a Negro, so we always had one on the grand jury."

"Don't you know, Mr. McDonald, that there is now and has been through all these years, such a prejudice against Negroes that a Negro cannot get a fair and impartial trial in this county?"

"No, sir. I don't think that is true. We are always fair to the Negroes here."

"Isn't it true that you never heard of a white man in all of your life being convicted in this county for killing a Negro? And don't you know that there have been many white men who have killed Negroes in this county and gone unindicted?"

"Well, I do not recall anyone being convicted, and I guess there have been some who have killed Negroes."

"Don't you know it to be true that of the two Negroes who have killed white men in this county during your lifetime, both of them received the death penalty and were hanged right out on this courthouse yard?"

"Well, I guess that's true."

In this manner, the trial of Harry Lacey began. Lacey, a Negro from Trinity County, was charged with the murder of Edgar Womack, a prominent Trinity County rancher. There was no question that Lacey was drunk when he killed Womack one moonlit night in February while he was on his ranch near Apple Springs. Lacey was not a tenant of Womack's, but he owned a little farm adjacent to Womack's ranch. As far as the record went, the two men had always been on friendly terms.

Bosey Beasley was a white lowlife who lived in the same community. Womack had suspected that some of his hogs were being stolen and that Beasley was doing it. About 9:00 or 10:00 p.m., Womack went down to the branch where he found a washpot full of boiling water and one of his hogs, which had been killed and was being prepared to be cleaned. Everybody had fled the scene, and Womack called one of the Negroes to carry the hog on his back up to his residence, where he intended to dress it. As they approached the house, with the Negro with the hog on his back walking in front—and Womack following— all at once a shotgun roared in the moonlight. Womack died almost immediately.

A posse was organized in the community, and the search for the assailant began. They went to a Negro woman's house, and she said that Harry Lacey had come there about an hour earlier at a high run, asking if she had any shotgun shells. He had appeared to be greatly excited and drunk and had told her that he had already killed one of the white SOB's and was afraid he was going to have to kill some more. This, of course, pointed to Lacey as the murderer. All of the forces were united and bent on apprehending him. He was discovered the next day down in a river bottom. Since Womack was a very promi-nent man in the county and excitement over the matter was running high, the sheriff thought it expedient to take Lacey to the Huntsville jail—about 30 miles away—for safekeeping.

At that time my brother, Reginald S. Bracewell, was practicing law in Huntsville in partnership with Ernest Wright and was a candidate for district attorney. The primary election was to be held in July. Reginald, of course, was aware that the case was loaded with political dynamite, but he needed the employment. So the firm of Bracewell & Wright agreed to defend Harry Lacey. They recognized that it was a very tough assignment, but that somebody had to take it.

The courts in that area were slow, and no one thought it probable that the Lacey case would be set for trial prior to the July primary. But, as so many times happens in a thing of that kind, the unexpected came about. The trial was scheduled to begin about July 1, with the political primaries to be held the last Saturday in July. There were four candidates in the race, and Reginald suspected that politics had something to do with the unusually expeditious setting. Having a death penalty imposed on his client wouldn't do a candidate for prosecuting attorney any good.

The indictment was returned promptly in Trinity County, which lay in the same judicial district as Grimes. Excitement in that county was running so high that the judge transferred the case to Grimes County on his own motion. I was practicing in Houston at that time, but I was not overwhelmed with work and seeing Reginald caught in this predicament, I volunteered to take his place in the firm representing Lacey in order that he could be free to carry on his campaign for district attorney. Although the compensation was quite small, I became entangled in the case which was destined to be drawn out four years—almost to the day.

Having been born and reared in Grimes County, I was keenly aware of the history of the White Man's Union and how difficult it was to obtain a fair trial for a Negro there, especially when he was charged with killing a white man. I suffered no illusions that Lacey could escape the death penalty should he go to trial in Grimes County and knew my only hope of saving my client's life was—to more or less—wear the case out. It occurred to me that there probably would be reversible error in the court's overruling a plea to change the venue of the case out of Grimes County. That was why I opened with the interrogation of Mr. McDonald.

Lacey's story was that he encountered Bosey Beasley and that Beasley gave him a drink or two of corn whiskey (this was in the days of Prohibition) and induced him to help him kill Womack's hog and dress it. After the two men had killed the hog and begun preparations to clean it, they heard Womack coming and ran and hid in the bushes while Womack took the hog away. Beasley then told Lacey he would have to kill Womack in order to escape going to the penitentiary for having stolen the hog. Beasley had a gun, and Lacey also had a gun. Beasley threatened to kill Lacey if Lacey didn't kill Womack. Under this threat, Lacey stationed himself with Beasley along Womack's pathway home. With his gun in hand, Beasley stayed off a distance behind a post while Lacey fired the fatal shot.

The weakness of the story lay in the fact that it was a bright moonlit night, and there was no convenient place for Beasley to hide while he exercised duress on Lacey—that is, put Lacey in fear of his life unless he took the life of Mr. Womack. Lacey persisted in his story to the end, and the true facts will never be known this side of eternity.

The defendant's story was not, strictly speaking, a defense against the charge, since if he and Beasley went into the unlawful enterprise of stealing the hog and the outcome was such as Lacey said it was, they would both be guilty of murder. But Beasley had not been indicted for murder; he had been indicted for the theft of the hog and had been acquitted. The defense theory was that he had not been indicted on the more serious charge because he could be used more effectively as a witness if he were not under indictment and that the State had never expected to indict him. We thought if we could show that Beasley was a participant in the crime and the State was deliberately refraining from indicting him, the sense of equal justice which exists among the American people would keep Lacey from receiving the death penalty. In fact, that was all that we lawyers hoped to accomplish in his representation—it was the best that Lacey himself hoped to get.

For some reason, S. W. Dean, the judge of the 12th District—which includes both Grimes and Trinity counties—disqualified himself from sitting in the trial of the case so the trial was held before Judge W. C. Davis, an eminent jurist noted for his fairness. Since the venue already had been changed once from Trinity County to Grimes County, I hardly hoped that it would be changed again to some other county on account of racial prejudice. The main purpose of the motion to change venue was to lay the predicate for an appeal. The expected happened, and the case was ordered to trial.

The selection of the jury was a long and tedious process taking two full days. I was acquainted personally with probably half the veniremen and knew their politics and prejudices fairly well. I disqualified quite a few of them, but a lawyer is allowed only 15 preemptory challenges in a death penalty case. In a case of this character where prejudice is so deep seated and some would actually be eager to get on the jury to see that the defendant got "speedy justice," the preemptory challenges go very quickly. By the time ten of the jurors had been selected, all of my challenges were gone. From there on, it was up to me to disqualify them or they would be taken over my protest.

One of the last veniremen—after my challenges had been exhausted—was John D. Rogers, a very prominent planter in Grimes County who had many Negro tenant farmers on his place. It so happened that one of them had escaped from Rogers' farm in Harris County while Rogers was claiming that the tenant owed him considerable money. In fact, I had agreed to defend the Negro in Harris County and to do my best to defeat the claim. I surmised that Rogers not only had a prejudice against a Negro charged with killing a white man, but that he also had a prejudice against me. After a lively bout of about 20 minutes, Mr. Rogers most commendably told the judge that he did not believe that he could make a fair juror and asked to be excused. I relate this to show what I was really up against.

With the jury finally complete, the trial started. The testimony established the facts more or less as I have detailed them, as well as Womack's total innocence of any offense toward anybody. His being wronged by the theft of the hog as a prelude to the wanton killing made a most discouraging case for the defense. The second morning when I began the defense testimony, word came that the daughter of one of the jurors was desperately ill in Houston and had to undergo an emergency operation. There was nothing for the judge to do but declare a mistrial so that the juror could rush to Houston to be with his daughter. I breathed a deep sigh of relief because I knew so many of the jurors that I felt like a quick death penalty had been certain.

The case did not come up again for about three months. In the meantime, my brother was successful in his race for district attorney and, of course, having put my hand to the plow, I had to go through with Lacey's representation. The second trial was very much a repetition of what had been started in the first one. We resubmitted the motion for a change of venue and agreed that the same testimony that was introduced in the first trial could be introduced and made part of the record in the second. This shortened the preliminaries to quite a degree.

The same hassle was made over the selection of the jury. While I had an unsatisfactory jury the first time, when we had completed the selection for the second trial, I wondered if I would not have been better off had we gone on through to the end in the first attempt. The prosecution was headed by a special prosecutor by the name of Cleo McClain of Conroe, a former district attorney known for his effectiveness. I had ascertained that he had Bosey Beasley summoned—someone had pointed him out to me. A more loathsome and despicable-looking character I never saw. Although the district attorney had Beasley under subpoena, I was fearful that he would not put him on the stand and thought it would help us considerably if I could contrive some means of forcing him to do so. So I interrogated every witness McClain put on as to his acquaintance with Bosey Beasley. The interrogation usually went about as follows:

"Isn't it true that you know Bosey Beasley, who lived out there in that community?"

"Yes, sir."

"Isn't it true that you have seen him around here in attendance in the courtroom since you have been here?"

"Yes, sir."

"Isn't it true that you saw him while he was talking to the district attorney?"

"Yes, sir."

"I'll ask you to state if it is not true that the district attorney took Bosey Beasley into the witness room and had a caucus with him."

"Well, I don't know. I saw him go into the room with Mr. McClain."

After I had asked about the third witness this same line of questions, Mr. McClain got up and assured the court that such interrogation was not necessary as he was going to put Bosey Beasley on the stand. When he did, he naturally had to interrogate Mr. Beasley as to whether or not he stole Womack's hog. Beasley denied it strenuously, saying, "I was tried in Huntsville for stealing that hog, and the jury found me not guilty."

I very casually rose and told the court that we objected to the question and answer and moved to strike it out as hearsay, because it was getting before this jury what the opinion of the other jury was as to whether Beasley stole the hog.

The judge said, "I overrule your objection. Gentlemen, proceed with the trial."

My heart almost leaped within me because I felt like I had something to stand on in the appellate court. As it turned out, it was a life-saver. I put Lacey on the stand to tell his story, and he made a fairly good witness testifying with great earnestness how Beasley forced him to kill Womack. However, the State came back with the woman who testified that Lacey came to her house wanting more shells, stating that he had "killed a white SOB" and might have to kill another.

The jury wasn't out too long. They came in with a death penalty verdict in less than an hour. I thought the quickness of the verdict indicated prejudice in the jury and made it a point on the appeal.

When the Court of Criminal Appeals received the case, they were not entirely satisfied with it because they are very careful in a death penalty case to see that the defendant has had a fair and impartial trial. They seized upon Beasley's answer about being acquitted for hog-stealing and ordered the case back for a new trial. Judge Davis had very few reversals in his long and distinguished career and was somewhat chagrined at this one. He did not want to try the case again and transferred it to Montgomery County.

It was about the same thing in Montgomery County, where the case was tried three or four months later, led by McClain as special prosecutor, District Attorney William Barron of the 12th Judicial District, and Mr. Pitts of Conroe—who was at that time district attorney. It was a long, hard fight. I discovered before I got through that Montgomery County was probably harder than Grimes County—as far as prejudice against a Negro accused of killing a white man was concerned. We finished the charge and made the argument to the jury, who got the case about 10:30 at night. I had been treated quite fairly by the bar in Conroe, and many of the citizens seemed more or less sympathetic. I had borne down so hard on Bosey Beasley, both in introducing Lacey's testimony and in my argument to the jury, that I was very hopeful of a life sentence. The jury was out about 30 minutes and rang the bell. The bailiff came in and told the judge something, and I knew they had reached the verdict—the death penalty. It was so soon.

The bailiff went back, and the clock ticked on for another hour without another sound in the courtroom. It was probably the most tension-filled hour I have ever experienced. At about two minutes after midnight, the jury filed in and read the verdict of guilty and assessed the punishment of death. I crept up to the judge and asked for an explanation of why there had been a full hour from the ringing of the bell until the jury came in. He said that the jury had sent him word that they had reached a verdict, but wanted to report right after 12:00 so they could get an extra day's pay for serving.

Again we appealed to the Court of Criminal Appeals, and they gave the case a very exhaustive investigation and decided to affirm it. We then applied to the Supreme Court of the United States for a stay of execution to get a certiorari.

Judge Hugo Black granted a stay of execution, but the certiorari was denied. The case ended in the execution of Harry Lacey exactly four years to the day from the time he was arrested.

◆◆◆

Thank You For a Life Sentence[2]

"KIRBY ALLEN, stand up. You have been charged by indictment in this court with the offense of murder and robbery with a deadly weapon. Do you have a lawyer to represent you?"

"No, sir," replied Allen.

"Why do you not have a lawyer to represent you?"

"Your honor, I have no money with which to hire a lawyer."

"That being the case, it is the duty of this court to appoint one or more lawyers to represent you. Knowing from the record that you have heretofore not been represented by a lawyer, I have given the matter some thought and decided to appoint two young men of this bar to represent you. They have practiced law in this court and are very diligent and faithful. I therefore appoint Russell Wolters and J. S. Bracewell. Do you accept them as your lawyers?"

"Yes, sir."

The foregoing conversation between Judge Neal Robinson and defendant Kirby Allen was a preliminary to a very interesting criminal case. It posed the question: Can an honest lawyer wholeheartedly defend a guilty man? My kin and well-wishers around Sand Hill and Mount Pleasant had asked that question over and over. As far as I was concerned, my defense of Kirby Allen—a somewhat notorious hijacker in the Houston area in the early 1920s—gave them their answer.

This case proved for all time how easy it is for a lawyer to acquire a sort of sympathy for the vilest criminal. While he may not desire to see him set free, the attorney feels like throwing in everything he has to mitigate the situation of the wrongdoer—if nothing more, to save him from burning in the electric chair.

[2] From a Manuscript of J.S. Bracewell.

From a lawyer's standpoint, a worse situation could not be imagined than that of Kirby Allen. He was a Negro man about 40 years old without a family or close relatives. He was charged with murder and robbery by firearms. He had already served two terms in the penitentiary. And, of course, as he told the judge, he had no money or property of any kind.

Under the laws of Texas, it was mandatory in all cases where the death penalty might be imposed that the court appoint one or more lawyers to represent the person charged. The judge was elderly Neal Robinson, who was able, fearless, and relentless in his pursuit of wrongdoers. He almost single-handedly broke up the operations of the Ku Klux Klan in Houston and Harris County.

In those days, such court appointments carried no compensation whatsoever, not even any expense money. Because of this, there is a widespread, erroneous assumption that a defendant under these circumstances does not get the highest type of service. This notion is far from the fact—especially where the lawyer is worthy of his license. First, he knows the defendant is without money and without friends. This ought to prompt the lawyer to be diligent. Second, the lawyer knows the judge had faith and confidence in his integrity and in his capacity to do a good job or he would not have appointed him. The lawyer considers himself a special representative of the court and is anxious for the judge to feel that the defendant had every legal right protected, especially where the death penalty may be inflicted.

So it was with this feeling of responsibility that Wolters and I—both in our late 20s—took up the defense. We first obtained newspaper accounts of the crime and learned that it had been most revolting. An old man lived alone and operated a little grocery store in Houston's Fifth Ward. He would close up about nine o'clock each night, carefully putting the receipts for the day in a little safe under the counter and then go to bed in a small apartment at the back of the store.

On the fatal night in question, while the old man was placing his money in the safe, the villain crept into the store, killed the old man by striking him on the head with a piece of iron, and escaped with the small amount of loot. An Italian, whom I will call Tony, claimed he saw a Negro emerging from the store at a run—soon disappearing down the sidewalk. Tony went in and found the old man and gave the alarm.

Police officers put on a citywide search for the murderer, arresting numerous suspects and taking them down to the city jail for quizzing and fingerprinting. Since Tony was the only one who claimed to be an eyewitness when the murderer escaped, he was carried down to the city jail each time to look over the suspects. After scrutinizing seven or eight, he finally fastened on Kirby Allen, the defendant, as being the man he had seen coming out of the store.

There are only two defenses in a case of this kind: one—an alibi; the other—insanity. Allen claimed he had an alibi. He said he was at the home of a Negro woman playing cards at the time of the murder. Another Negro woman was there at the time, and upon our investigation, they both verified Allen's story. The weakness of the case was that he left the card game about the time the crime was committed, and it was obvious that the district attorney could argue effectively that he left the card game and immediately went and committed the crime.

The case had attracted considerable attention, particularly among the Negroes, and everyone expected Allen to get the death penalty. We felt reasonably certain that there would be a large crowd in the courtroom—predominantly Negroes. We decided that our only hope of saving the defendant's life was to weaken Tony's identification of Allen, knowing that Tony would stick by his stated opinions to the very last.

The district attorney—to make the proof of death by deadly weapon—called Tony to the stand, where he related very vividly how he was coming down the walk when Allen rushed out of the store. Tony said he got a good look at him and could not be mistaken in his identification. The harder we tried to shake him, the more tenaciously he stood by it. My cross-examination of him went something like this:

> "Now, Tony, you were carried to the jail on numer-
> ous occasions to identify suspects of the crime,

weren't you?"

"Yes, sir, I was."

"Now, with each one of those suspects, you looked them over very carefully, did you not?"

"Yes, sir."

"The truth of the business is, you looked each one of them over far more carefully than you did Allen as he ran out of the store, didn't you?"

"Well, sir, I sure did."

"In fact, you didn't have nearly as good an opportunity to observe Allen as you did those suspects at the jail, did you?"

"No, I didn't. That's right."

"Now, I suppose, Tony, if I were to bring one of those suspects before you now, you could identify him just the same as you did Allen, couldn't you?"

"Yes, sir, I sure could."

"And you wouldn't be mistaken about it, would you?"

"No, sir, I sure wouldn't."

"Now, would you please get up from the witness stand and walk to the railing here and look over these people sitting on the two front rows of seats and pick out the one who was brought before you as a suspect. If more than one were, point out as many as were brought to you at the jail."

Tony felt sure that he had been trapped, but he couldn't back up. He knew that we had planted some of the suspects out in the audience and were going to show that he couldn't identify them, although he had observed them so much better than he had Allen. He walked to the right and then to the left. He finally pointed his finger at one of the men in the second row and said, "That's one of them right there."

The Negro Tony had identified as a suspect was so bewildered and confused that he jumped up and left the courtroom—to the amusement of the jury and the audience. It was the general feeling that Tony had made a bad error and that the Negro he pointed out was nothing more than an onlooker at the trial.

When order was restored, I got up and very solemnly asked the court to issue an instanter subpoena and have the sheriff bring the fellow back to court and hold him as a witness—the implication being that I would show that he had never been carried to the jail at all. But the sheriff couldn't find the man and what he would have said was left as an unanswered question in the trial.

Of course, we could not put Allen on the stand. After we had put on our alibi witnesses—all of whom were very weak—we had to rest the case.

In the argument, Wolters and I bore down on the weakness of Tony's identification and ridiculed his testimony, saying essentially that he could not identify any of the suspects of whom he got a much closer view than he got of Allen.

Notwithstanding, everybody expected a quick death penalty. The jury was gone about two hours and came in with the verdict: "We, the jury, find the defendant guilty as charged and assess his penalty as life imprisonment in the penitentiary."

Allen, who had fully expected to burn, leaped to his feet and shouted, "Thank you, gentlemen. Thank you."

Needless to say, my conscience didn't bother me.

Mr. Wolters advised me that he checked on Allen some 15 years later and found that he had served honorably in the pen and had been released on parole in 1945.

◆◆◆

The Trial of Tom Pasco

"NOW, MIKE [that was the policeman's name], would you mind lying down on the floor before this jury and showing them just how the dead senorita was holding those scissors when you found her body?"

"To be sure, Mr. Williford. I will be glad to do just that for you."

The policemen all swore by Williford, the prosecutor.

Such was the dramatic moment in the trial of Tom Pasco. He was a Latin American about 25 years of age. He had choked his beautiful wife to death after they had been married only about a year. The officers found her in her apartment, dead, with bruises about her neck and a pair of scissors in her hand. The State's theory was that Tom entered their room about nine o'clock at night while she was working on a garment, and in a jealous rage—thinking that she had probably been out on a date—seized her by the throat and strangled her to death. It was the theory of the defense that Mrs. Pasco was extremely jealous about Tom and that since he had been out that evening far beyond the usual time of his return, she was seized by a jealous frenzy when he entered the room. In her hand, she had a pair of scissors which she had been using to prepare a garment. Suddenly converting the scissors into a weapon of force, she lunged toward Tom. He seized her by the throat in self-defense without any intention of taking her life, but she was strangled to death before he actually knew what was taking place.

The way Mrs. Pasco was holding the scissors when the officers and others of the household found her body became an extreme, hotly-contested issue. Since the defendant had not previously disclosed his line of defense, the prosecuting attorney apparently did not realize the importance of this detail when he put on the first part of his case. He showed by questioning the undertaker that she was dead and—through the doctor—that given the marks on her throat and the condition he found her in at the inquest, she in all probability met her death by strangulation. The prosecutor also put on the officer, Mike, and others to show the condition the body was in when they found it.

On cross-examination of all these witnesses, the defense bore down upon the matter of just how she was holding those scissors. Quite obviously, if she was using the scissors as a deadly weapon to kill Tom, she would more than likely have the point down to and below the lower part of her right hand in a more or less striking position. The State's witnesses were not very certain on this detail of the case. Some thought she had the scissors in one position and some in another, but all emphasized that she had been choked to death while she was apparently tending to her duties as a housewife in mending her husband's garments.

Tom Pasco was a quite well-educated young man who was very high-strung and could have been taken very readily for an artist of some kind. He stated that when he returned home, his wife became extremely angry and jealous, berating him for not having come home earlier, and seized the scissors in her hand as she would have a dirk knife and lunged toward him. He had no means whatsoever of protecting himself other than to seize her and try to take the scissors away from her. At the time, it occurred to him that the best way to do this was to take her by the throat and choke her until her hands released the scissors. He was quite dramatic in his recounting of the events; however, due to the fact that he was of normal size and she was a small girl—weighing probably less than 100 pounds—as an excuse for taking human life, it didn't make the strongest story.

However, Tom was quite certain that was the way she proposed to use the scissors—and his brother and father who hastened to the scene were equally certain that when they found the dead body, the scissors were in that position in her hand.

Mr. Williford, who later occupied the same court bench (Judge Frank Williford) with distinction, sensed the importance of the position in which they found the scissors in her hand when they reached the body. During the court recess, he evidently had a conversation with some of the State's witnesses, particularly Mike. After Mr. Williford had refreshed their memories, they were quite certain that Mrs. Pasco had the scissors pointed between her thumb and her index and middle fingers, not downward in a clenched hand as Tom had stated. After we had concluded our testimony and the case had gone back to the State for rebuttal, Mr. Williford recalled Mike to the stand and requested that he lie down before the jury and put on the demonstration mentioned above.

As Mike stepped down from the stand to sprawl on the floor before the jury, Mr. Williford handed him the scissors and asked that he demonstrate their actual position. Once down on the floor, Mike, who was known as a brave, fearless officer, became confused by the unusual proceedings—somewhat to the amusement of the jury.

Mr. Williford said, "Now, Mike, how was she holding those scissors?"

Mike took the scissors in his own clenched fist and held the point down, exactly as the defense was contending it had been. Mr. Williford said, "Now, Mike, you evidently didn't understand my question exactly. I mean for you to show the jury how those scissors were pointed in the hands of this young woman when you discovered the body."

Mike said, "It was just this way."

And try as he could, the prosecuting attorney never did get Mike to change his story. So the testimony ended on that climax—or to the district attorney, that decided anticlimax. Of course, the question of how Mrs. Pasco was holding the scissors was not the controlling piece of evidence because, considering the relative size and position of Tom and his wife, it was not likely that he was put in deadly fear for his own safety—even if the scissors were pointed down. But there had been so much emphasis given to the matter in the testimony and Mike had explained it so dramatically that it evidently was the turning point in the case.

The jury was out approximately two hours and came in with their verdict to a very tense courtroom—with my heart almost leaping through my throat. The verdict read: "We, the jury, find the defendant guilty of murder as charged, but we further find that he has never been convicted of a felony in this or any other state, and we recommend that his sentence be suspended."

Of course, the suspension of the sentence was mandatory under the law, and Pasco immediately obtained his freedom.

There is an interesting sidelight on this case about the fee. It was during the dark Depression, and the lawyers were taking cases for about what they could get. The boy's father was a very humble old Mexican, and he was brought to me by a friend of mine named Southerland. The case had been so publicized that the father thought his son was certain to get the death penalty, and so did Mr. Southerland. Old Mr. Pasco had no money, and Southerland was going to advance him the down payment on the fee.

After some sizing up and some speculation as to what the fee should be, we settled on $2,000 with the payment of $200 down. I felt quite sure that Southerland had agreed to lend Mr. Pasco the $200. A person seldom receives any payment on a criminal fee after the work is done. The old man assured me that if I could save the boy's life, he would be thoroughly satisfied, and he knew that I would have an uphill fight in doing so. The case was tried within about 30 days after I accepted the employment. I had received no further payment on the fee up until that time. Of course, the family was overjoyed at the results and said they expected to pay the balance of the fee as soon as they could, but I had heard that story so many times that I paid very little attention to it.

One rainy night—while my wife, our two children and I were at home—there was a knocking at the back door. I thought it was some black people who wanted to get their neighbors—who'd been arrested for gaming—out of jail. When I opened the door, to my utter amazement, it was Tom Pasco's father. He pulled out a roll and counted out to me the $1,800 balance due on the fee. While I was dumbfounded at the verdict in the case, I cannot say that I was half as dumbfounded as I was when the old gentleman handed over the balance of the fee.

In the practice of criminal law, that happens only in dreams.

◆◆◆

The Punch-Drunk Bandit

ONE HOT JULY day during the 1930s—at about three o'clock in the afternoon—a bandit armed with a pistol entered the Thom McAnn shoe store in downtown Houston, held up the cashier, and departed hurriedly with a negligible amount of money. The streets were crowded and, before long, there was great excitement. Soon, police officers took up the chase and cornered the bandit down on the banks of Buffalo Bayou in the vicinity of the Grand Central Railroad Station. A battle ensued in which one of the officers was shot in the arm—but once the bandit had emptied his pistol, there was nothing for him to do but surrender and be taken into custody.

A few weeks prior to this incident, there had been a rash of holdups and burglaries in Houston, and the officers were being criticized for their inability to do anything about them. This holdup was the boldest and most irritating of all. It seemed to be an opportune time to vindicate the officers by making an example of the perpetrator.

The grand jury was in session, and the next day it returned an indictment against the bandit named Emmett George, charging him with three counts: one of robbery by assault and two of assault with intent to murder a police officer. Under the laws of Texas, the defendant must be served with a copy of the indictment, and the case may not be set for two full days after he is so served. Once the indictment was served on George, the district attorney immediately asked the court to set the case three days hence. The district judge ordinarily follows the recommendation of the district attorney in such cases, and the trial was set accordingly. The D.A. might have sought the death penalty if George had been charged with robbery by firearms, but a special jury panel would have been required—meaning a month's delay, which was why he was able to avoid the more serious charge.

The case was very brief. Through questioning the store manager, the prosecutor showed the facts of the holdup and the identification of Emmett George as the bandit. Once the prosecutor brought out the chase by the officers and the shooting of the officer, the case was complete. George took the stand in a state of confusion and frustration and began weeping. A lawyer by the name of F. O. Fuller happened into the court-room at that time, saw the defendant weeping, and offered to represent him if the court would permit him to do so and would give the attorney a little time to ascertain more about

George's background and any facts that might mitigate his crime.

While the court refused any sort of postponement, it did permit the lawyer to sit in on the case as George's representative and ask him some questions to develop a few facts, one of which was that he was only 17 years of age. After being out only a few minutes, the jury brought in their verdict of guilty on all three counts and assessed George's punishment at 40 years in the penitentiary.

A newspaper reporter was in the courtroom and wrote up the proceedings in a more or less dramatic fashion. One of the afternoon papers carried the news under glaring headlines to the effect that a 17-year-old boy had been assessed 40 years' imprisonment in the state penitentiary. The story further showed that it had all been done on the fourth day after the offense, without the defendant being represented by a lawyer. While public sentiment had been quite hostile toward that type of crime, the reaction was one of immediate sympathy for the boy. The newspaper carried statements from some prominent people as to the inhumanity of the proceedings, all of which were calculated to put the judge and district attorney in a bad light. Instead of softening them up any, the reports had just the reverse effect. They were more determined than ever to make an example out of George.

At this juncture, a welfare association headed by a Mrs. Bloomquist and a Mr. Gustafson became interested in the case and enlisted my services in doing what I could to mitigate the sentence. Mr. Fuller filed a motion for a new trial, and one was set for only two days off, which was the day following my enlistment. My first appearance and plea to the court was to postpone the motion for a new trial in order to give a little more time for preparation for the hearing.

It had been ascertained after the trial that George's parents both lived in Atlanta, where his father was a streetcar motorman. George had just graduated from high school in Atlanta. Since employment conditions there were bad, the boy had decided that he would come to Texas as a land of opportunity. He had made fairly good grades in high school and had attended a Methodist church and Sunday school in that city regularly. I represented to the court that all of this made it so unusual for a boy to commit a crime like that—under the circumstances which he did—and that it required further investigation.

The judge was adamant and refused to order any postponement of the motion for a new trial, at the same time giving a lecture on the necessity of curbing crime in Houston and also making a pass or two at a lawyer who would come in and try to defend a criminal under such circumstances. I became quite angry and argumentative myself, referring to the fact that this was a good boy from a distant city who had fallen into evil ways and was being railroaded to the penitentiary. This remark was very unfortunate on my part because the judge reprimanded me severely and threatened to put me in jail for contempt of court.

Since the public was already aroused, all of this made very interesting stories for the newspapers, and I suddenly found myself somewhat of a heroic champion of the underdog—with public opinion on my side. The motion for a new trial was quite promptly overruled and I gave notice of appeal, which helped keep my client from being taken to the penitentiary since he had to stay in jail pending his appeal. The proceedings, of course, were not in any shape for an appeal as I had not had time to prepare all the documentary material which would be necessary to go into the record in such a case. While the procedure was somewhat rare, we ascertained that the law authorized a second motion for rehearing, particularly in cases where there was a show of insanity as a possible defense. With this precedent to go on, Mr. Fuller and I prepared an elaborate second motion for a new trial, setting forth all the previous proceedings and alleging that there was insanity in the family and that the boy was highly nervous and impulsive. Furthermore, we pointed out, he had become an expert boxer in high school and had engaged in amateur prizefighting. We noted that shortly before he left Atlanta, he had taken part in a prizefight and had gotten severely mauled and that there was a form of insanity prominent among prizefighters that was known as "punch-drunk."

When it was all ready, we presented the case to the court and asked that it be set down for a hearing, since we wanted to introduce evidence to support the allegations of the motion. The motion was set down as it indeed had to be. By the time it came up for hearing after a few days, Mrs. Bloomquist and her associates had raised the money to get the defendant's parents to attend. The parents were good, hardworking, poor people, and I doubt if they had ever been out of the city of Atlanta in their lives. We put the father on the stand, and he verified all of the allegations in the motion. We, likewise, put the mother on the stand, not so much for the allegations of the petition, but in order to create human interest background for the stories the newspaper boys were writing. Our supreme hope was that by force of public sentiment, the judge and the district attorney would relent to the extent of granting a motion for a new trial and would give our client the minimum of five years under a plea of guilty. Under such an arrangement and with good behavior, we could have had him out and back home in a little less than two years. But all of this was of no avail. Our motion to be allowed to file a second motion for a new trial was overruled, but we had the record in such shape that we thought the court of criminal appeals would have a reasonable basis for sending the case back for a new trial.

One of the defects of the Texas system of criminal jurisprudence is that when a defendant receives a sentence of more than 15 years in the penitentiary, he cannot—under any condition—be allowed bail pending his appeal. While the rule is sound for most cases, it certainly ought to have some leeway whereby bail could be granted in cases such as this. But George had to stay in jail during the ten months we waited for his appeal to be decided. In the meantime, he became antagonistic toward the jailers and had a fight with one of the inmates and was kept in solitary confinement for a good part of the time.

The court of criminal appeals judge knew me well enough to know that I would not willfully misstate either the law or the facts in any case—not only from the standpoint of personal integrity, but from the standpoint of policy in the case on trial. Everyone should have known that the court would not decide on the case without examining the facts disclosed in the motion for a new trial, as well as all of the law pertaining to the case cited by the brief. When the court indicated to Mr. Branch that it did not relish his statement, he became completely angry and frustrated and remarked, "Well, if the court wants us to try it again, we can try it again," and sat down.

This part of the story may have had a bearing on the second trial. Of course, the sole issue was that of insanity. Unfortunately, under the laws of Texas, the judge will charge the jury that if the defendant knew the difference between right and wrong, insanity is not a defense and he is responsible for the commission of the crime. Everyone knows that most people in the insane asylum—and most idiots that could be found—would know the difference between right and wrong, and yet it is ridiculous to think of one of them being punished criminally for doing something which they knew to be wrong.

After the prosecution had made its case, which was necessarily brief, it devolved upon the defendant to make the case of insanity. Mr. George, the father, testified as to the strains of insanity in his family, two of his aunts having been in the insane asylum and some of his other relatives having become insane— all of which was verified by Mrs. George, the mother. We then put on a couple of managers of boxing exhibitions who knew all about prizefighting. They testified that when a fighter had fought as George had and had undergone the punishment which he had, he would often become both mentally and physically upset, and that this condition was known among the prizefighters as "punch-drunk." While the State made strenuous objection to these gentlemen expressing an opinion upon Emmett George's insanity—as far as knowing right from wrong was concerned—the court admitted it, and they testified that they doubted very much if he knew the difference between right and wrong at the time he committed the offense.

Lay witnesses are entitled to express an opinion about a person's sanity. In that connection, we used Mr. Fuller—the lawyer who happened to be in the courtroom at the time George was testifying in his first trial. Mr. Fuller testified that the boy was not talking coherently and did not seem able to pursue any connected train of thought and that—in Mr. Fuller's opinion—he did not know the difference between right and wrong. This led to a rebuttal statement by Mr. Branch, who had conducted the first trial and also knew George's demeanor on the stand on that occasion. Fuller and Branch got into an altercation over what the real facts were, and the lawyers threatened to draw their knives and have it out in the courtroom. However, the judge exercised an effective restraining influence and the case was quieted down. In its rebuttal, the prosecution used several psychiatrists, all of whom testified that in their opinion, George was sane at the time he committed the offense, certainly to the extent that he knew the difference between right and wrong. They also said that he was conscious of his wrongdoing at the time he robbed the store; this was shown by his flight and his attempt at protecting himself by shooting the officer.

After the prosecutor got through with Dr. York's (one of the psychiatrists) interrogation for the state, I propounded this question to him: "Now, Dr. York, assuming that this boy was 17 years of age at the time of the offense, that he grew up in the city of Atlanta with poor parents and made his way through high school making fairly good grades; that he also was a constant Sunday school attendant and was never known to violate any law; assuming further that he was given to expert boxing and had engaged in a very strenuous prizefight soon after he graduated from school and was severely beaten up in such fight; that after the fight he left home without telling his parents where he was going and with the little money he had, purchased a cheap pistol and thumbed a ride to Houston—a distance of more than 1,000 miles; that he took the pistol at three o'clock in the afternoon and walked into a shoe store in downtown Houston and held up the manager of such store at that time and place; that he escaped into the crowded streets of the city of Houston and in his flight shot two officers; and assuming further, Doctor, that he was from a highly-nervous family and two of his aunts had been in the insane asylum and another kinsman had died in the insane asylum—if you knew these facts, Doctor—without having known any other facts—would you say that at the time he robbed the store he was sane or insane?

After considerable hesitation, Dr. York said, "Well, I believe you have described the acts of a crazy man and that he was probably insane." Of course, this looked like a quite substantial concession, but the prosecution took him back on reexamination and through devious questioning and emphasis on some of the facts, particularly that of the escape, Dr. York stated that he believed the boy knew right from wrong. This was about the condition of the testimony on which the case was closed.

Judge Whit Boyd charged the jury upon the question of insanity as directed by the higher court to the effect that if they had any reasonable doubt as to George's sanity or insanity to the extent that he did not know right from wrong at the time he committed the offense, they should acquit him.

While we were fairly hopeful for an acquittal, it was a little too much to ask the jury to go that far. They more or less compromised their verdict by giving Emmett George five years in the penitentiary.

In view of the long wait for another appeal to the Court of Criminal Appeals and the strong probability that the case would this time be affirmed, we decided to accept the sentence and try for an early pardon. Mrs. Ferguson was then Governor of Texas and was known for her sympathy toward people in the prison system. After Emmett George had been there approximately two years, Mrs. Bloomquist, Mr. Gustafson, and others, including myself and Mr. Fuller, decided it was worthwhile to apply for a pardon. One unvarying requirement of the pardon board is that there must be obtained from the trial judge a statement of his view of the case.

In light of Judge Boyd's attitude about the case—both the first and the second trial, and the criticism he had undergone—we figured that it would be absolutely impossible to get a favorable recommendation out of him but, nevertheless, decided to get his statement in line with the board's policy—even though it were unfavorable—and try to overcome it in some way. When I took the matter up with Judge Boyd, I was somewhat astounded at his most generous and sympathetic approach to the matter. He said, "Why, sure, Bracewell. This was a bad boy, and I knew it. I have received a lot of criticism on account of the case, but I believe that he has had his lesson, and I am glad to join in a recommendation for a conditional pardon."

I omitted to say that at the conclusion of the second trial when George stood up to be sentenced, the judge asked him if he had anything to say as to why the sentence of the law should not be pronounced against him. To the very embarrassment of Mr. Fuller and me—as well as his father and mother—he said, "Well, judge, you are a big man and a righteous man here, but when you get to hell, you are just going to be a common sinner like the rest of us." Apparently, Judge Boyd had forgotten his remark.

While visiting the City of Atlanta some 15 years after this, I found Emmett George listed in the telephone book. I went out to his house. He was still living with his father and mother, who were old and decrepit and in a most distressing situation. Emmett had conducted himself properly and was the manager of a grocery store and making a fairly good salary. It may be that Judge Boyd was right after all and that the boy had served just about enough time to straighten him up and make a good citizen out of him.

◆◆◆

The Strange Case of Elmer Williams

IN THE EARLY 1930s, the city of Houston was shocked by the brutal murder of an Italian woman by the name of Margiotta. She and her husband ran a grocery store in the Fifth Ward. One evening at 9:00 p.m.—about closing time—a Negro walked into the store and shot her down in cold blood, stripping the cash register and fleeing. Her husband was about the store at the time the crime happened, but it was done so quickly that he hardly knew what was going on. He saw the assailant run from the store, but was not able to pursue him. He gave the alarm, but it was some 15 or 20 minutes before the police officers got there, and the assailant had time to make a clean getaway.

There was a heavy Italian population in the area, and the murdered woman was one of fairly large acquaintance and influence. The papers carried big headlines about the crime, and law enforcement officers scoured the city for a week or more without finding a likely suspect or one that Mr. Margiotta could identify for certain as being the murderer.

About three weeks later, it was reported that a Negro by the name of Elmer Williams had been arrested in a small town in Ohio and had made a complete and detailed confession of the crime. The details were such that there just could not be any mistake about it. The officers rushed up to Ohio and brought Williams back to Houston. Since he had made a confession in such convincing detail, Mr. Margiotta had no trouble whatsoever in identifying him as the party who had killed his wife. It looked like a death penalty case if there ever was one, and the wealthy Italian citizens made up a handsome purse and employed Jo Edd Winfree—a prominent criminal lawyer of the city—as special counsel in the case to assist District Attorney Horace Soule, who was also an experienced prosecutor.

An indictment was brought down very speedily, and the case was set for about three weeks off. Since Williams had no money or friends, Judge Neal Robinson appointed St. John Garwood and me to represent him. Garwood was a brilliant young lawyer who later became an Associate Justice of the Supreme Court of Texas.

In a case of murder with robbery as the motive, there are only two possible defenses, one being insanity and the other an alibi. Because Williams confessed and was identified by the dead woman's husband, we ruled out the alibi defense and there was nothing left to go on but the defense of insanity. Having that defense in mind, as soon as Williams was brought to Houston, the prosecution engaged the city's three leading psychiatrists to examine him as to his sanity. This placed us at a disadvantage since all of the others were of lesser reputation. Once they had examined the defendant, the three prosecution psychiatrists very promptly announced that they found him fully sane and capable of committing the crime.

Although the defense of insanity was going to be an uphill

proposition in view of the opinions of the three psychiatrists, it was the only thing left for Garwood and me. We went down to the jail to probe into the defendant's background and into his past experiences, insanity in the family, or any other phase that we might look into. We had a long, fruitless interview with the defendant along that line, and we seemed to get nothing to cling onto. It looked like a hopeless proposition.

As we prepared to leave the jail, Williams said, "By the way, would you gentlemen be interested in an alibi?"

The question interested us not so much because of the possibility of an alibi, but as evidence of mental derangement in the defendant.

We said, "Oh, yes. But why ask? Do you think anybody would be willing to believe any testimony of an alibi in view of your certain identification and confession?"

"Well," he said, "if you would be interested in an alibi, I would like to tell you my story. I figured all the time I would get a life sentence for this, and I didn't mind going to the penitentiary for the balance of my life; but from what I hear, I think I'm going to get the electric chair, and I don't want that."

"Then what is your story about your alibi?"

"Well," Williams said, "I have read the indictment, and I know I was in an insane asylum in Beatrice, Nebraska, when the crime was committed and for a few days after."

We felt certain that this was a hallucination and might furnish a possible key to the defense of insanity.

"Well," we said, "you may have been insane, but you have proven to be a fairly good liar, too. If you were incarcerated in the insane asylum in Nebraska at the time the crime was committed, how on earth could you have made a detailed confession of the crime—describing it as it actually happened?"

"Now, listen," he said. "I had been in that insane asylum for several years, and I was tired of it. A few days after the date named in the indictment, I decided to escape. I ran away and got in a boxcar of a freight train and left Beatrice. When I got into the boxcar, I found a Negro who seemed to be very much in trouble. He told me that he had shot an Italian woman in Houston, Texas, and was afraid that he was going to be arrested and carried back for trial. He said there was a pretty fair defense in the case since the Italian woman was making at him with a gun. He described the thing to me so thoroughly that I got it in mind, then he offered me a hundred dollars if I would confess to the crime and go back and take the rap for him. I had never been to Texas, but I knew it was nice and warm down there, and I decided that I would rather spend the balance of my life in a Texas penitentiary than go back to Beatrice to the insane asylum. When we got to the next town, we got off and I went to the officers and told them that I was the person they were looking for in Houston and that I had committed the crime.

"After I had done that, the other Negro immediately left, and I didn't get a cent for it. When I got to Houston, I was taken out to the place and was positively identified as being the man who killed the woman. Then I heard them talking about it and found out they were going to give me the electric chair. I just didn't want to go to the electric chair. Now, I want to make this defense of an alibi if you gentlemen will go with me on it."

We said, "But who in the world would believe your story? Is there anybody anywhere who will say that you're telling the truth?"

"Well," he said, "the superintendent of the asylum in Beatrice knew me well, and he will testify that I was in the asylum at the time of the crime."

By this time Garwood and I were so thoroughly bewildered that we wanted to think this astonishing development over. We went back to the office and, after a conference, decided that it was worth a call to the Beatrice Insane Asylum to talk to the superintendent. To our utter amazement, the superintendent verified Williams' story and said that Williams actually was there in the asylum at the time of the murder and that his record would verify that fact and the date of his escape. The superintendent also stated that he would come to Houston and bring his records with him if we could arrange to pay his expenses. After some difficulty we raised the money and arranged for him to come down.

We wanted to keep our defense a secret and spring it like a bombshell during the trial. The district attorney got a little

suspicious at our maneuvers and especially over our not inter-
viewing psychiatrists. He went down to the jail in our absence
and bore down on Williams as to what his story was going to
be. Williams told it to him, and Mr. Soule likewise telephoned
Beatrice, Nebraska, to talk to the superintendent and find out
his story. To his astonishment, the staff at the asylum told him
that the superintendent was on his way to Texas to attend a
criminal trial. That fairly well revealed to the district attorney
what our strategy was.

The case was called the next day. Amid a crowded courtroom, the judge called on the State for an announcement.
They stated that there was an important witness in attendance
that they wanted to talk to, telling the judge that he was from
the insane asylum in Beatrice, Nebraska. The judge insisted
that we give the prosecution permission to talk to our witness.
After a long conference with the superintendent and reviewing
his records, the prosecution decided that there could be no
answer to the alibi. The district attorney and the special prosecutor came back into court and announced that they were not
ready and wanted time for further investigation.

We told the court that we were ready and had gone to
considerable expense to get the witness here. We also said that
the district attorney had more time to investigate than we had.
The district judge sided with us and ordered the case for trial.
With great chagrin and embarrassment, the district attorney
and the special prosecutor announced to the court that they
had decided that Williams was not the murderer and they
wanted to dismiss the indictment.

The act caused great astonishment and headlines in the
newspapers. As a kind of face-saving expedient, the district
attorney went to the county court and filed a charge of insanity
against Williams, asking that he be held under warrant for a
trial to be later sent back to the asylum at Beatrice, Nebraska.

With a rather ghoulish satisfaction, Garwood and I entered
an appearance for Williams for the insanity trial and summoned
the three psychiatrists who had publicly pronounced him sane.
When the prosecuting officers saw that they would be defeated
by this maneuver, they dismissed the complaint of insanity,

took Williams about 12 miles from town, and put him out on the highway. So far as I know, he was never heard from thereafter.

Our only compensation came from the remarks of Judge Robinson from the bench. He praised Garwood and me very liberally for the work we had done in the case and admonished the law enforcement officers and told the crowded courtroom that it was a dangerous thing to try to rely upon a confession and that so many times identifications go wrong. He said that even the most skeptical should now be convinced that the lowliest demented Negro—without money or friends and a thousand miles from home—could have his rights protected the same as the man with ample resources to prepare the most skillful defense known to criminal law.

◆◆◆

The Defense of Roy "Pete" Traxler

ROY PETE TRAXLER was a contemporary of Clyde Barrow and Bonnie Parker, Pretty Boy Floyd, John Dillinger, and the other desperados who terrorized the United States in the early 1930s. While Traxler said he knew them and knew of their operations, he always swore that he was not among them. Yet he held the unchallenged title of "Oklahoma's Public Enemy Number One" and had a long and notorious record of crime.

Traxler began his career in crime at the age of 14 years. He served terms of confinement in a number of juvenile institutions—as well as the Oklahoma penitentiary. He was also accused of several murders and robberies for which the authorities lacked the evidence to convict him. He married a woman named Nell, who aided and abetted him in his crimes and remained loyal to him for many years after the events on which this narrative is based.

Not satisfied with his exploits in Oklahoma, Pete Traxler went down to Texas and held up a Lipscomb County filling station at gunpoint. He was captured and charged with robbery by firearms. Although Traxler was wanted on several charges of murder and robbery in Oklahoma at the time of his arrest, the Oklahoma authorities , who were tired of contending with him, decided to leave it to Texas to handle him since he was charged with a capital offense and would probably get the death penalty or confinement to the penitentiary for life. (At the time, robbery by firearms was a capital crime.) Shortly before Traxler's arrest, the Texas law had been changed to permit a guilty plea and a life sentence in anything less than a capital case. But in all capital cases it was necessary to impanel a jury to pass upon the accused's guilt or innocence and to fix the penalty. Wanting to make quick work of the matter, the Lipscomb County District Court immediately appointed a lawyer to defend Traxler and set the case for trial.

Since there was no death or bodily injury inflicted during the robbery, the district attorney and Traxler's lawyer agreed that a jury probably would not give him the death penalty. The District Attorney agreed to reduce the charges to robbery by assault and allow Pete to plead guilty and take a life sentence, thereby eliminating the time-consuming process of calling a jury. But since the law was new, it had not been fully construed, and there was no court order entered in the minutes reducing the charge from robbery by firearms to one of robbery by assault. After Traxler had spent eight or ten years in the Texas prison system, this point became highly important.

Following his sentencing, Traxler was transmitted to the penitentiary at Huntsville. After a few weeks—and although he was frail and not used to hard work—he was sent out with a gang at the Eastham Farm to work in the fields hoeing and plowing cotton. This prison farm was located in the Trinity River bottom, and the heat was so oppressive as to be unbearable. Resourceful Pete Traxler had kept up an underground communication system with Nell, and before too long she had smuggled two or three pistols and a rifle down to the farm and told Pete where they were hidden. He took two other prisoners of desperate character in on the deal with him. They worked themselves down the cotton rows within reach of the guns, seized the weapons, disarmed the guards, and fled. Taking over the first farmhouse they came to, the three paused for a bath, changed into whatever clothes they could find there to fit them, and made plans for their getaway.

When the Huntsville sheriff—who was 20 miles away—heard of the escape, he dispatched two brothers, Deputy J. C. Dunlop and Constable Howell Dunlop, to take up the trail and capture the fleeing convicts. It so happened that the house Pete and his cohorts had taken over belonged to one of those officers. The Dunlops arrived there quickly, and a fierce battle ensued inside.

Traxler was a crack shot, as were the other two desperados. He shot the guns out of the Dunlop brothers' hands. Then he shut the officers up in the house, took their guns and ammunition, seized their automobiles, and headed northeast toward the Oklahoma line at a terrific rate of speed. All East Texas was aroused, and posses were organized in the various counties to catch the convicts. But the prisoners eluded all the lawmen and made it to Oklahoma. Avoiding filling stations, they commandeered cars and engaged in pitched gun battles for about a week. One of the three prisoners was killed and another wounded. Finally, Traxler ran out of gas near Madill, Oklahoma, and barricaded himself behind some trees. After several exchanges of shots, being worn out, sleepy, hungry, and out of ammunition, he surrendered to the officers, who took him to Durant, Oklahoma, and put him in jail.

The escape and ensuing manhunt had received wide publicity. Although Oklahoma had several charges—capital and otherwise—against Pete Traxler, the authorities there decided to surrender him back to the Texas courts. The authorities figured that if he were tried in Huntsville on charges of robbery by firearms for taking the guns from the Dunlops, he would be certain to get the death penalty. Two such robbery indictments were filed against Traxler: one that he did "then and there forcibly take and steal from J. C. Dunlop a pistol of the value of $25 with the intention to then and there appropriate the same to his own use and benefit;" the other that he seized and took, "with the intention of appropriating the same for his own use and benefit," the pistol of Howell Dunlop.

Although my brother, Reginald Bracewell, was the elected district attorney of Walker County, of which Huntsville is the county seat, public sentiment in favor of giving Traxler the death penalty was so strong that Governor Allred announced that he was employing the Honorable M. E. Gates of Huntsville as a special prosecutor for the State. Gates had a long and successful career in the practice of criminal law and was regarded as one of the best in Texas.

Nell Traxler went to see my brother's former partner, E. R. Wright—a Huntsville attorney—who had become my intimate friend. He asked Nell for a fee of $2,000. She agreed, but couldn't come up with more than $200 for a down payment. The Depression was still on, and lawyers were having a hard time eating. Besides, it was a reasonably attractive case for a young lawyer such as Wright, because of its wide publicity. Upon the payment of the $200 and promise of another $800 within a few weeks, Wright accepted the case.

When Wright attended the examining trial, the prosecution's determination to win the death penalty made the young defense attorney feel that he needed a more experienced lawyer to share his heavy responsibility. So on October 15, he phoned me in Houston, knowing that lawyers there were having a hard go of it—probably harder than they were in Huntsville. Our conversation went about as follows:

"Hello, is that you, J. S.?"

"Yes, sir."

"This is E. R. Wright of Huntsville."

"I see you've been having some excitement up there."

"Yes, sir, and plenty of it."

"I hope you're not mixed up in it in any way, E. R.," I said, suspecting that he had probably been engaged to defend Pete Traxler.

"Yes, sir, J. S., I'm just mixed up in it head over heels. I'm really behind the eight ball, and I need your help."

"Well, you know I've never turned you down yet," I replied, "but this is a pretty hard assignment."

"I know, J. S.," he said. "But Traxler's wife came over to see me and wanted to employ me. Someone had to do it, so I just took Traxler's case. Since then, you know, the Governor has employed Mac Gates to help Reginald with the prosecution—in fact, take over the prosecution. They're going to set the case down and give me the rush act and send Pete right on to the electric chair. What I mean is, I need some help and I need it bad."

"Well, E. R., I suppose the fee arrangement is entirely satisfactory, knowing that not one criminal in 25 ever has anything to spend for defense."

"Traxler's wife has been over here and paid me $200," he declared. "And she's promised the balance of $1,000 on the $2,000 fee Monday a week, when the case is set for trial."

"Wright," I said, "you just tell Nell for me that she is a big liar. I've been in this business now 15 years, and I've never yet collected a fee in a case like this after I did the work."

"Nonetheless, J. S., I really believe she'll pay the fee. She has some property up there in Oklahoma, and she's going to sell that to pay us."

"Well, Wright, I'll do anything for you," I said. "And of course, that goes for helping you in the defense of Pete Traxler. As far as Nell and the $1,800 are concerned, I think we might as well forget it."

"I hated to call upon you, J. S. But my back is to the wall, and I surely would appreciate it if you'd help me."

"About all I can say, my friend, is that I will be there. So long."

That's the way I got hooked up in the defense of Roy Pete Traxler, the most notorious case—either civil or criminal—that I have ever been connected with.

Huntsville is only 70 miles from Houston. While the trial was set a week from the time I talked to Wright, I made it a point to go up beforehand by jitney bus to discuss the case with him and lay the courtroom strategy. There was only one issue in the case—namely, whether or not Roy Pete Traxler should be given the electric chair for the crime he had committed. The prosecution and the defense both recognized this to be the only issue. The escape and capture had generated such wide publicity that the public generally knew about all the other charges that had been brought against him, apart from the robbery of the Dunlop boys.

Since Traxler already had a life sentence in the Texas prison system hanging over him, it would profit the State nothing to give him another life sentence. There was not much danger of injuring Traxler's reputation, and another life sentence wouldn't hurt him in the least. Thus, the issue was drawn. It was really going to be a fight unto death.

E. R. Wright was not only a most capable lawyer, he was also a wonderful judge of human nature and gauger of public sentiment in a community. While the case had received wide publicity, he sensed that there was a deep-seated prejudice in Huntsville and the rest of Walker County against the whole prison system. Within the past few months there had been stories of guards beating prisoners unmercifully and of the unbearable living conditions down on the Eastham Farm. Of course, the prison system exercised quite a political influence in a place like Huntsville, particularly on the townspeople; so it became all-important for us to know something of the jurors' prejudices for or against it.

We had been served with a copy of the list of special veniremen. Since each side was entitled to ten preemptive strikes (strikes without assigning a reason), our first job was to analyze the list thoroughly. To my surprise, Wright not only knew everyone on it, he knew their politics as well.

In view of this fact, the next issue to determine was whether we would ask for a change of venue—that is, to move the trial out of Huntsville. While we thought our chances there would be better than they would in some of the adjacent counties, nevertheless, we decided to make the motion, anticipating that it would be overruled and we would have this point to use on appeal. Our next gambit would be to ask for a delay, alleging that we believed Pete Traxler was partially insane and that we would need considerable time to explore the matter of his possible impairment and get up the evidence with reference to it. Further anticipating that this motion for delay would be overruled, we planned to emphasize the unbearable conditions of the prison system and the desire of all the prisoners to escape from it. We further planned to ask the Court to charge the jury that if they thought that Traxler took the pistols away from the officers for the purpose of effecting his escape—rather than believing beyond a reasonable doubt that he'd taken the guns for the purpose of appropriating them for his own use and benefit—they should acquit him. We thought, too, that we might throw in the issue of insanity after we had talked to Traxler's mother, whom neither of us had ever seen or communicated with previously. If she indicated that there had been any insanity on either side of the family, we'd get an issue and a charge on insanity.

Such was the strategy we outlined in our preliminary conference.

Promptly at 9:00 a.m. on Monday, Wright and I entered the courtroom. He announced that I would be chief counsel for the defense, and my brother announced that Mr. Gates would be chief counsel for the prosecution. The bailiff called a long list of jurors, and the Court qualified them. Since it appeared that enough jurors were present to proceed with the trial, the judge, Honorable Max M. Rogers, called on the State to declare itself ready or not ready. The prosecution promptly announced ready for trial. It was then that the bailiff brought in Pete Traxler in handcuffs. This was the first time I'd ever laid eyes on him since I saw no use for any preliminary conference with him.

Wright and I then told the Court that we wanted to file a motion for a change of venue due to the fact that the case had so much publicity in Walker County and it had been widely publicized that the governor had entered the picture for the purpose of obtaining a death sentence, all of which made it serve the ends of justice to transfer the case to another county. This motion was very promptly overruled.

We announced to the Court that Mrs. Hesbrook, the defendant's mother, had just arrived from Rush Springs, Oklahoma, after traveling all night and that we desired to talk to her at length to ascertain if there was insanity in the family and if that might be a possible defense. The Court granted an hour for that interview. At the end of that time, with the court reassembled and the courtroom filled with prospective jurors, I asked for leave to make a formal application for a continuance.

Since everybody except the defendant and his lawyers wanted the show to go on, Judge Rogers invited me to dictate the motion to the court reporter in open court.

After the preliminaries of the motion, I continued my dictation, saying that the mother of the defendant was not in good health and had traveled all night from a distant town in Oklahoma to attend the trial and that the defense lawyers had not had time to interview her except in the brief interval that the Court had allotted to us. I added that during that time we had ascertained from the mother that—when she was 14—she had married Traxler's father, who was a drunkard and a dissolute character, that he had abandoned her and she had never heard from him since, and that Traxler had never seen his father. I said that we had also learned that shortly after Pete Traxler's birth, she had married again and her second husband had acquired an early prejudice against the boy and had treated him most cruelly as a stepchild. The stepfather beat Traxler unmercifully and continued such a course of cruelty that the boy became an epileptic at the age of nine. After the stepfather's brutal treatment drove Pete Traxler from his home at the age of 14, the boy had become an outlaw from society and had engaged in a career of crime ever since.

I was somewhat eloquent in telling my story to the court reporter, and Mr. Gates got up and objected to my manner of dictating the motion, since there were many jurors sitting in the courtroom. He asked the judge to either restrain me or have all the prospective jurors withdraw. The judge promptly sent the jurors outside the courtroom. This action didn't help the prosecution any, because those jurors already had become interested in the story. I continued my dictation, saying that the train of events connected with Traxler's epilepsy and his almost continuous career of crime since its onset raised the issue of insanity. I added that we were not prepared to develop that issue on such short notice and asked that the case be continued a reasonable time until we could prepare and present such a defense at the trial. The Court overruled the motion and ordered the trial to proceed.

Texas gives a very wide latitude to a lawyer in examining

prospective jurors on a venire list. Attorneys are many times criticized for their waste of time, but this is their way of getting acquainted with each prospect and sizing him up as to his prejudices or lack of prejudices and his suitability as a juror.

This case offered a fruitful area for the practice of that art. After ascertaining where the juror lived, how long he had lived there, his acquaintance with the Dunlop brothers, and his acquaintance with Mr. Gates and my brother Reginald, we passed on to the prison system, asking how much the prospective juror had observed of it and whether he had formed any prejudices as to its operation. We then went into the facts of the crime, determining whether the prospect had read about it in the papers and had kept up with the long case of Traxler through Texas and Oklahoma and with his capture. We also sought to find out whether all of this had caused the prospective juror to form an opinion as to our client's guilt or innocence. By reason of such searching questions, we were able to disqualify many whom we did not want.

We always wound up with this question and with considerable emphasis: "Mr. Blank, this indictment charges that this defendant 'Roy Pete Traxler forcibly and with a firearm took from J. C. Dunlop a pistol of the value of $25 with the intention of appropriating the same for his own use and benefit.' Now, the Court will charge you upon the law of the case as it is submitted to you, and if he should charge you that the pistol must have been taken with the intent of appropriating the same for the defendant's own use and benefit, if he should further charge you that if you believe from the evidence that Traxler took the pistol from Dunlop for the purpose of effecting his escape and not for the purpose of appropriating it to his own use and benefit, or if you should have a reasonable doubt on this point, you should acquit the defendant. Now, Mr. Blank, if the Court should so charge you to that effect and you had a reasonable doubt as to whether Traxler took the pistol only for the purpose of effecting his escape and not for the purpose of stealing it, would you follow the Court's charge and acquit the defendant?"

Naturally, all the jurors whom we took declared themselves wholly committed to that proposition. The older I have become in the practice of law, the more I have become convinced that a lawyer should begin the argument of his case upon the examination of the jurors.

We had two or three challenges left when court adjourned for the day, and the next man on the list was a Christian preacher—pastor of one of the local churches. It had always been one of my cardinal principles never to take a preacher, a song leader, or a peace officer on the jury in a criminal case. Wright and I had quite an argument about what we were going to do about this Christian preacher who was to be called the next morning. I, of course, was opposed to taking him and violating my main principle of selecting a jury in a criminal case. On the other hand, the preacher was Wright's friend. Wright knew him well and was so fully convinced that he would make a good juror for us that I finally said, "All right, but Pete Traxler's blood will be on your hands." Little did I suspect that this preacher would become the foreman of the jury and would be a strong influence in our behalf.

About 10:00 a.m., with the jury impanelled and sworn and the plea of "not guilty" made, the State began introducing its testimony. The prosecution made a rather vicious case with the testimony of the Dunlops—who had been greatly injured, one with a bullet wound—and of some of the officers engaged in the chase. Two of the lawmen were brought down from Oklahoma to identify Traxler as the man they'd arrested and returned to Texas. There was not much we could do in cross-examining these witnesses, because any cross-examination would only make bad matters worse.

The prosecution rested its case about noon. Then we had to decide whether the defendant should give any testimony. In our case, we decided without much difficulty that we would not put Traxler on the stand because of all his previous convictions, which we did not care to air out. After our motion for postponement, the judge and the prosecuting attorneys fully expected that we would put Mrs. Hesbrook, Traxler's mother, on the stand to detail his background and raise the issue of insanity. On the other hand, in describing all the activities of the escape, we thought we had fairly well raised the issue of whether the seizure of the pistol was for the purpose of theft or for the purpose of escape.

The indictment alleged that the pistol was worth $25. The issue of whether it was necessary to prove its value is a question that might be argued among lawyers, but Mr. Gates did ask Dunlop what he considered the pistol worth, and he said $25. It was introduced in evidence. It was a very plain-looking pistol—to the uninformed, at least, it was hard to see how that sort of pistol was worth $25. Again we let the matter rest right there without trying to cross-examine because we figured that if we weakened Dunlop's testimony as to what the gun was worth, the State could call quite a few peace officers who were hanging around and greatly bolster the allegation of the pistol's value.

All in all, we decided to rest our case without introducing any testimony and go to the jury on the intent with which the pistol was taken. In presenting the matter to the judge in chambers, all agreed to submit the charge on the intent with which the pistol was taken, a point that had been settled clearly in Texas and would undoubtedly have constituted reversible error had the Court not granted it. (I used this point again ten years later in defending Traxler in Durant, Oklahoma, where the Court refused to do so. The Supreme Court of Oklahoma backed up its previous decisions and held that the failure to grant it was not reversible error.)

We then approached the matter of a charge on the value of the pistol. This was more or less an afterthought. We stated to the Court briefly that it was a well-known rule that the State—though it makes an immaterial allegation—must prove any allegation it lays in the indictment, and if the State was required to prove the allegation, we were entitled to have a charge on it—that is, a charge to the effect that the jury must believe beyond a reasonable doubt that the value of the pistol was $25 or they should acquit the defendant. It was quite evident to everyone that as the matter stood the jury was either going to give our client the electric chair or turn him loose, and the Court's charge didn't make a lot of difference. The learned judge said he would give the charge and so incorporated that feature into the trial.

It didn't take long to prepare the charge. By 2:30 p.m., we were ready to argue the case to the jury. My brother, Reginald, made a quite forceful argument for the prosecution, relying on the undisputed facts and ridiculing the idea of considering the intent of anyone returning the pistols to the Dunlops. Wright reviewed the prison system, the conditions existing there, and the pistols that Traxler owned and could get. Wright argued that the circumstances under which the pistols were taken in the gun battle at the house absolutely precluded any thought of theft in Traxler's mind at the time. I took very much the same line and was followed by Mr. Gates making the closing argument for the State. I have heard him argue many cases, and I believe that he made the most vigorous and inflammatory argument in this case that I have ever heard him make. When he finished, it seemed to nearly all of the onlookers that it was the foregone conclusion that Traxler would get the death penalty and in short order.

That was the atmosphere in the courtroom when the jury retired.

After the jury had been out about an hour, they rapped on the door. Everybody thought that was it. The sheriff took the judge a note which had been written by the foreman, the Christian preacher. The note asked the judge to send in the pistol, and the bailiff carried it to them. After about another hour, they again knocked on the door—this time they had reached a verdict.

It is a most solemn thing to sit in a courtroom in anticipation of a death penalty verdict. There was an oppressive silence as the foreman handed the verdict to the venerable clerk, Mr. Tindell, and he read it as follows:

"We, the jurors, find the defendant not guilty."

Everybody was so completely flabbergasted that they just didn't know what to say. The judge said, "I doubt if either the State or the defendant can obtain a fair trial on the other indictment pending here for the robbery of Howell Dunlop. Therefore, the Court is of its own motion transferring such indictment to LaGrange, the county seat of Fayette County." Nobody thought that the judge's announcement amounted to anything, because Traxler already had a life sentence hanging over him. No one thought the State would go to the expense of sending him to Fayette County, and Fayette County would not be inclined to undergo the expense of coming to get him and going through a trial.

We all thought it advisable to keep the defendant inside the walls of the penitentiary rather than in the Walker County jail, and the bailiff telephoned the warden to come get Pete Traxler and take him back to prison. While the warden was on his way, Wright and I walked over and congratulated Traxler, who was very nervous and chain-smoking cigarettes. Wright said, "Pete, the Lord has been very good to you, and you owe it to Him and to everybody connected with this trial to make a model prisoner. Furthermore, Pete, if you will conduct yourself honorably and never violate any rules or regulations of the penitentiary, we will—after you have served five years— undertake to get you your freedom."

I joined in, pledging that if Traxler would do as Mr. Wright had asked him, I would try to help him regain his freedom after five years. Traxler quite readily agreed. In this manner, the most sensational trial that I have every participated in ended.

The significance of the promise which Wright and I made can only be understood by following the fortunes and misfortunes of Roy Pete Traxler a little further in his checkered career.

◆◆◆

The Fortunes and Misfortunes of Roy Pete Traxler

AFTER THE TRIAL of Roy Pete Traxler in Huntsville in November 1937, there was hardly anyone who didn't think he would soon conduct another prison break and probably get killed outright or commit a robbery or murder while trying to escape and this time receive the death penalty. He just could not be so lucky a second time.

I was building up a sizeable practice in Houston handling a growing volume of tax litigation. In 1939, I was elected President of the Houston Bar Association. My fellow local lawyers had an ambitious program of reform in court procedure that they wanted to carry through the next term of the Texas Legislature, and they gave me a very busy year.

One of my best clients was Parker Brothers & Co., Inc., producer of oyster shell, which they dredged from Galveston Bay. In the fall of 1939, World War II broke out, and Governor O'Daniel—apparently seeing that the United States would be dragged into the conflict sooner or later—began a giant defense program. Oyster shell had become a defense commodity. Because it was approximately 90 percent lime, it began to be used in the manufacture of cement, fertilizer, chicken feed, and magnesium. Besides this, it was a principal surfacing material employed in establishing the large military encampments in and around South Texas.

There were three large producers of oyster shell: Parker Brothers, W. D. Haden & Co., and Horton & Horton. The Army was recruiting at such a rate that manpower was getting pretty scarce, and I soon had the responsibility of representing the entire shell industry, particularly in its relations with Washington and the defense program.

Wright was elected to the legislature, and after a distinguished career there, he was elected superintendent of the Texas School for the Deaf. Such were the years from 1937 until 1943. Pete Traxler had been entirely forgotten.

One day I received a letter from Pete, who still appeared to be incarcerated. He reminded me of the promise that Wright and I had made to try to get him out after five years if he could show a course of exemplary conduct in the meantime, and he enclosed a copy of his record demonstrating just that. When I inquired of the prison officials directly, they confirmed that Pete Traxler had been a model prisoner since 1937.

Since Mr. Wright was an official and an employee of the State of Texas, he could no longer participate actively in the case, but I communicated with him about it, and he assured me that he would cooperate in every way possible. We agreed that it was up to us to make our word good. Traxler was penniless; his wife had abandoned him and married someone else. To her credit, though, within a few months after the trial in Houston, she had sent Mr. Wright the entire $1,800 she had promised. It had been derived from the sale of some of her property. Regardless of any compensation that might be involved, I felt some obligation to do what I could to obtain a mitigation of Pete's punishment and, if possible, to win his release.

Traxler was clearly eligible for parole under the laws of Texas, so I decided to take his case up with the Board of Pardons and Paroles in Austin and see if they wouldn't parole him in view of his record of exemplary conduct since the prison break. I happened to be personally acquainted with the members of the parole board. Since Pete had no friends to recommend him, about all I could do was to show his clean prison record. The trouble with that record as it appeared in the prison certificates was that it showed seven or eight convictions and several charges still pending against him. Though quite friendly in a personal way, the Board of Pardons and Paroles told me that they just could not possibly grant any concessions whatever to a man who had a record like that. In fact, they closed the door to any further application for a considerable period of time.

Something prompted me to write to the district clerk of Lipscomb County asking for a copy of the proceedings there in which Pete had been given his life sentence. When the record came, the only irregularity I could find in it was the fact, that faced with an indictment on a *capital* offense (in those days, robbery with firearms was a *capital* offense—such is no longer the case), Traxler had waived a jury, pleaded guilty before the judge and been sentenced by the judge. Traxler remembered that there was conversation in the courtroom during which it was agreed orally that the charge should be reduced to robbery by assault. It was a matter of *jurisdiction*—that is, the power of the judge to accept the plea of guilty and impose the sentence in a capital case—it being necessary that a jury was necessary in a capital case. The question presented was whether or not the record—that is, the judge's docket sheet and the Judgment of Conviction itself—should not show affirmatively that the district attorney reduced the charge from a capital offense to one of robbery by assault and, therefore, gave the district judge jurisdiction to try Traxler without a jury. Upon examination of the question, I decided that it was worthy of presentation to the Court of Appeals. If the judge did not, in fact, have jurisdiction to accept Traxler's plea and sentence him without a jury, unless or until the charge was reduced, the conviction was void and he was entitled to release. Only matters of jurisdiction can be presented on behalf of a convict after his sentence has become final.

I prepared the application for a writ of habeas corpus and presented it to one of the district judges in Houston. His sole function was to ascertain the facts and make the application returnable to the Court of Criminal Appeals for a ruling on the question.

The Court of Criminal Appeals was fully aware that deciding the question in Traxler's favor and ordering his release would have the effect of opening the prison gates for many convicts who had been sent there under exactly the same circumstances. However, the proposition was sound, and the Court quite courageously sustained it. The report of the case is cited in *Ex Parte Traxler*, 184 S.W.2d 286 (Tex. Crim. App. 1944). While they held that the Lipscomb County conviction was void and that Traxler was entitled to be released from the penitentiary, they further ruled that the indictment was good and that setting aside the conviction did not mean setting aside the indictment, which was therefore still pending. They ordered Traxler to be remanded to Lipscomb County to stand trial again on the original charge. Wright and I had anticipated this, but it presented no problem, since we had previously ascertained that the man who had been robbed had sold his filling station and moved and that his whereabouts were unknown. The State, therefore, could not prove that the offense was committed against the will of the complainant.

Wright and I fully believed that Traxler had thoroughly reformed and that if we could obtain his freedom, he would not violate any law and might even make a useful citizen. The law enforcement officers of Texas, on the other hand, were thoroughly convinced that if Traxler regained his freedom, he would embark upon another crime spree, robbing and possibly murdering innocent people. Their position was completely understandable. Just what communications went on between the state officials, I do not know—but the District Court of Fayette County immediately issued a bench warrant to take Traxler from the penitentiary to LaGrange to stand trial on the Howell Dunlop robbery indictment, which had been transferred there by the judge on his own motion at the conclusion of the trial in Huntsville. They evidently thought that indictment would give them a much better chance of handing him another sentence and holding him than the one in Lipscomb County. The case was set for trial in LaGrange on February 1, 1945, which was about six weeks after the opinion of the Court of Criminal Appeals declaring Traxler's former conviction illegal.

Fayette County is populated largely by people of German heritage who are renowned for their belief in strict law enforcement. Moreover, the State was represented in that county by The Honorable Fred Blundell, who had held office there as district attorney for many years and was generally known to be a prosecutor who never lost a case. This, of course, made the situation look very bleak for us.

But the State was to have its problems in Fayette County, just as it would in Lipscomb County. Although we had made a motion for a change of venue in the J. C. Dunlop case in Huntsville, we did not make a similar application in the Howell Dunlop case. In fact, that case was not set down for trial. The law in Texas on change of venue is that if the State or the defendant makes application for a change of venue, it may be granted by the judge and the case moved to any county in Texas. It also provides that the district judge on his own motion may move to order a change of venue to any county *in his own judicial district or to any county in a district which adjoins his district*. It so happened that Fayette County was not in the Walker County district. Neither was it in a district which adjoined Walker County. It, therefore, appeared that we had a very solid basis for a motion to retransfer the case back to Walker County. We felt sure that our chances would be much better if we retried Traxler in Walker County rather than Fayette County.

And, too, eight years makes a tremendous difference in the way a person feels about a wrong. Howell Dunlop had long ceased to be a law enforcement officer, and he probably was well aware of the course of exemplary conduct Traxler had followed in prison since his Huntsville trial. In all likelihood, Wright had seen to this. The state allowance for mileage per diem for witnesses was wholly inadequate for their actual expenses, and since Dunlop would have had to spend several days in LaGrange during the trial, it was quite easy for him to find some reasonable excuse not to attend. Of course, his testimony was absolutely indispensable to the State's case, since the prosecutor would have to show that his pistol was taken from him against his will.

When the case was called in LaGrange, we made our motion to transfer it back to Huntsville in Walker County because it had been transferred on the judge's own motion and not to a county in an adjoining district. It was a little uncertain whether the point was good. We also knew that Dunlop had not arrived and that Blundell could not be sure his witness would get there in time to testify. The courthouse was crowded with jurors, and while Mr. Blundell was a great prosecutor, he was also quite politically minded and did not want the jurors to get the idea that the prosecution had slipped up on anything. Before making an announcement, he called for a conference with the defense lawyers and admitted in that meeting that, frankly, he thought the motion was good, but did not want it granted in open court and that he would use it as a basis for asking that the case be postponed and reset for some future date.

Naturally, we did not object. We reentered the courtroom, where Mr. Blundell—with great solemnity and impressiveness—stated to the Court that the defendant's lawyers had just filed a motion which was of more or less serious consequence. He added that he had no notice whatsoever of the motion and that while he recognized that the defendant was not obligated to file it in advance, that was the way such matters were usually handled. He went on to say that the State, without any lack of diligence or fault whatever on its part, had been surprised by the late filing of the motion. Despite all this, Mr. Blundell announced he thought that the intent of justice and correct procedure required that the case be postponed. Wright and I, of course, stood like sheep-killing dogs while Mr. Blundell said all this to the Court. At the conclusion of the statements, the judge entered the order continuing the case. Traxler was still required to stay in jail in Fayette County and could not get a trial of the cases either there or in Lipscomb County.

We then filed an application for a writ of habeas corpus before one of the judges in Harris County. After the hearing, the judge issued the writ returnable to Walker County and decreed in his order that after Traxler was tried in Walker County, if the Lipscomb County authorities did not send for him within 15 days, he should be released. Judge Rogers of Walker County entered an order sustaining Traxler's indictment and his order of transfer, but fixed bond at $2,500. When we appealed the case, the Court of Criminal Appeals held that the application for a writ of habeas corpus in Lipscomb County had to be made there *Ex Parte Traxler*, 148 Tex. Crim. 550, 189 S.W.2d 749 (Tex. Crim. App.—1945).

After these proceedings, the judge in Fayette County sustained the motion to retransfer the case to Walker County. The Dunlop indictment was sent back there, and we immediately posted the bond fixed by Judge Rogers. Upon our application to the Lipscomb County Court, the authorities there had agreed that no conviction could be made on the indictment there, and the case was dismissed. Now the only valid indictment remaining against Pete Traxler was the one in the Howell Dunlop case pending in Walker County.

Judge Rogers of Walker County knew of Traxler's clear record, and he also understood how difficult it would be to get a conviction in Walker County on that indictment. He wisely concluded that the case should not be set for trial, but further retained it in his court so that the indictment could be held over Traxler's head to insure his continued good conduct. Wright and I had become so thoroughly convinced that Traxler had reformed and would not only keep his word, but would not violate any other law that we personally signed his $2,500 bond, and he was released from the Walker County jail after having suffered continuous incarceration in jails and penitentiaries for more than eight years.

Mr. Wright got Pete a job with a construction company doing business adjacent to Huntsville. The wages were sufficient for him to pay his board and room and to reimburse us for some of the expenses we had incurred.

All went well for about five months. Then the company moved its operations to Denton, Texas, up near Oklahoma. Traxler continued his employment and his conduct as a law-abiding citizen, but word got across the Oklahoma line that he had been released from the prisons of Texas.

The matter became a political football in southern Oklahoma. The authorities there discovered that when Traxler had escaped to Oklahoma in 1936, he had taken an automobile from Mr. Trimmer and had driven it until it ran out of gas and then abandoned it. At the time, a robbery indictment had been returned against Traxler in Durant, and it was still pending. There was also a murder indictment pending against him in Madil, Oklahoma; the State could not sustain it, but Traxler had never been able to get it dismissed. The Oklahoma authorities issued warrants in Oklahoma and sent them to the sheriff of Denton County, who arrested Traxler on these old indictments. The question that immediately arose was whether Traxler could lawfully be extradited back to Oklahoma to stand trial on these indictments after a lapse of so many years.

After investigating the question, I was fully convinced that he could not, and we advised the authorities that they would have to get an extradition order from the governor. This led to a considerable hearing on this issue in the governor's office in Austin. In the absence of Governor Shivers, the hearing was held before Lieutenant Governor John Lee Smith. After wavering a bit, he decided to grant the extradition. We then had the right to apply to the Texas Court of Criminal Appeals for a writ of habeas corpus testing the lawfulness of the extradition.

We advised the Denton County authorities to that effect and immediately began to prepare the application.

As we understood it, Traxler was to be held for a reasonable time until we could present our application. The official apparently understood otherwise. Before we could get up there (approximately 300 miles), the Oklahoma authorities had appeared, and the Denton authorities had surrendered Traxler to them. They immediately carried him to Durant and lodged him in jail to await the setting and trial of the indictment there.

Pete Traxler managed to obtain local counsel, The Honorable Bill Steger—a quite capable lawyer—who immediately made application for bail. After a hearing, the Court granted bond in the sum of $5,000, which Traxler made through a friend by the name of Jones. Traxler thereby regained his freedom and returned to Texas. He went to Wharton about 60 miles south of Houston and found employment as a plumber. Upon my instructions, he immediately reported to the sheriff of Wharton County and gave him his full life history. The sheriff later became quite cooperative and sympathetic in the troubles that were to come.

◆◆◆

A Perspective on Roy Pete Traxler— from the Lawyer's Standpoint...

THERE IS AN element in the practice of criminal law which the average layman just cannot see: how a lawyer can become so zealous in the defense of a guilty man. The *Traxler* case is a fairly good example of this from the lawyer's standpoint. There is hardly ever a bad crime committed without a reasonable explanation. In this case, of course, the explanation was Traxler's background and the lack of any personal supervision or training on the part of a father. His stepfather was so cruel and inhuman as to drive Pete away from home at an early age. It would have been almost a miracle if a boy under those circumstances had not fallen into a career of crime. So, Traxler's background would naturally arouse the deep sympathy of any person with humanitarian principles. You come to feel that society—rather than the victim of such antisocial conditions as it permits to exist—is the real offender. On top of that, Traxler already had paid a rather heavy price for his evil conduct.

Since his 1937 Texas prison break, Pete Traxler had spent approximately nine years in the penitentiary. Texas had never, prior to Traxler's sojourn, received any honor citations for maintaining ideal penal institutions. One of the prime purposes of law enforcement is to reform the offender, but this result is obtained in all too few instances. After a lifetime in the practice of criminal law, I can say that Traxler furnished the best evidence in all my experience of a case in which the enforcement of the criminal law really effected the reformation of the offender. At any rate, the more determined the law enforcement officers of Texas and Oklahoma became to put Pete Traxler behind prison bars and keep him there for the rest of his days, the more determined I became to fulfill my promise and to see that he had a reasonable opportunity to lead a law-abiding life from then on.

I do not mean to imply any criticism of the law enforcement officers of Oklahoma. Pete Traxler had wronged their citizens grievously many times. On the other hand, it is easy to see how such a case could become a political football in state and local politics. After Traxler crossed the Oklahoma line in his desperate escape from Huntsville in 1937, he took a shotgun and held up Frank Trimmer and his wife, who were on the road peacefully carrying eggs and other country produce to market. He made them get out of their car and turn their backs while he drove it away. He continued to drive it while he was being hounded by the officers and—when it ran out of gas—he left it on the roadside and took somebody else's car. That was the basis of the indictment that was returned against him in Durant immediately after his capture and which had been pending all those years.

When it became generally known in Oklahoma that Traxler had gotten out of all his Texas convictions and was going about in perfect freedom just across the Texas line, it was very easy for an opponent of a district judge, sheriff, or district attorney to point to this undisposed indictment and criticize the incumbents for not taking appropriate steps to bring him back to Oklahoma and try him on that charge, as well as on the murder indictment pending in Medil.

From a legal standpoint, my position on the situation was as follows: after his 1937 Texas prison break, the State of Oklahoma had Traxler in its possession and sent him back to Texas to stand trial and be convicted, causing him to serve an illegal sentence of ten years in the penitentiary. By doing this, the Oklahoma authorities had waived their right to ever bring him back and try him there again. I made this contention before Acting Governor Smith in Texas and also before the trial court and the appellate court in Oklahoma. I was never able to sustain this point, and since it was a federal question, I hoped that if and when Traxler was convicted on one of these Oklahoma indictments, the United States Supreme Court would recognize that he had been denied due process of law and would order him freed.

My other theory, from a legal standpoint, was the same as it had been in the Huntsville trial—i.e., all the facts showed that Traxler took the property, not with the intention of depriving the owner of its use, but with the desperate intention of effecting his escape. This seemed quite obvious in the taking of Frank Trimmer's automobile in Oklahoma. The laws of Texas warranted that the Court charge the jury to distinguish between the two intentions. The judge in the Huntsville trial had done just that, and it had been a material factor in Traxler's acquittal. In Oklahoma, and based on several decisions, I concluded that the law was quite the same. (This was recognized in Traxler's first trial in Durant, but not in his second trial.)

Traxler stoutly maintained that he never thought of permanently appropriating Trimmer's automobile for his own use and benefit, but intended to take it only temporarily to aid in his escape—leaving it on the roadside when the gas ran out. Of course, nobody else knew or could know whether Traxler intended to steal the car or not. Since it was highly important that the jury believe that Traxler only intended to use the automobile to get away, I decided—as part of my strategy—to put him on the stand in Oklahoma and let him tell his own story. Then I would try to bolster his testimony by showing the reputation for veracity that he had built since he had been acquitted of his offense in Huntsville and also while he had been at large on bond since his release from the Texas prison system. I did this through a series of depositions. In this manner, I was trying to use Traxler's prison record to his actual advantage when, as an ordinary proposition, a prison record is almost fatal to a defendant who is being tried for a crime.

After Traxler's arrest and imprisonment in Durant on the Trimmer indictment, he was released on bond and returned to Texas to find work. He made it to Wharton, about 400 miles from the Oklahoma border and about 60 miles from Houston, where I was practicing law. We thought that with Traxler that far away, the people of Oklahoma would soon lose interest in trying him and imprisoning him further and, too, we figured that they would become aware of his good record and be content to permit him to pursue gainful employment as a free man so long as he did not molest anybody.

This approach worked out well for awhile, but finally the political angle began to work again, and the case was set for trial in Oklahoma. I went there with a lot of misgivings as a lawyer. I was not authorized to practice in Oklahoma, but it is an almost universal custom to permit a visiting lawyer to actively participate in the trial of a case outside his jurisdiction and even to take the lead in the trial. However, procedural details— particularly in criminal cases—vary from state to state.

About a week before I was to go up there and participate in Pete Traxler's trial, I ran across a cousin of mine by the name of Jim Bracewell, who had spent much of his life in Oklahoma as a peace officer. He had a malady that made it evident that he would not live very long, and he wanted me to draw his will for him, which I did. The circumstances were such that I did not feel that I should charge him for that service, and he begged me to tell him if there was not some way he could do me a favor in the short time he had left.

I said, "Well, Jim, do you know anybody in Durant,

Oklahoma?"

He said, "Indeed, I do. I've had a lot of business with the sheriff there by the name of Kirksey."

I said, "Well, I am going to Durant next week to try a robbery case. It's the case of Roy Pete Traxler, a man about whom you probably know something."

He said, "Hell! You're not defending that fellow, are you?"

I then told him something about my connection with the case and how long I had worked at it. I also informed him of Traxler's good prison record and my belief in his intentions to go straight in the future. Cousin Jim became very interested and said, "Searcy, I believe that I can help you some, and there's nothing that I would like to do more than to be of some help to you. I'll just call Kirksey right now about it."

Stepping to the phone, he called Sheriff Kirksey and told him that we were cousins and that I was going up there the next week to defend Traxler. Cousin Jim mentioned my having represented Traxler in Texas, Traxler's long stint in prison, and my full belief in his reformation. Jim said that he would treat it as a dying favor if Kirksey would help me in every way he could during this trial.

Kirksey and Cousin Jim were evidently warm personal friends because the sheriff made a ready response and promised to help me in every way he could, consistent with his duty as an officer. Sheriff Kirksey was a man of wide influence. He fulfilled every expectation and promise that he made to Cousin Jim and that was probably the reason I did as well as I did in the trial.

Being a regular churchman and a Sunday school superintendent, I thought it would not be out of line to go to church and Sunday School the day before we were to begin trial. There I discovered that Judge Sam Sullivan—the district judge before whom the case was to be tried—was president of the class, and the district attorney who was to prosecute the case was also a member of the class. This served to soften up the approach for me at the beginning of the trial the next day.

When the case was called, the prosecution announced ready for trial. I asked for leave to present my plea in abatement based on the fact that in 1937 the State of Oklahoma had complete possession of Traxler after his escape from the Huntsville penitentiary and his arrest in Durant and had voluntarily sent him to Texas to stand trial on a capital offense, thereby foregoing the right to ever return him and try him in Oklahoma on indictments existing at that time. I observed that quite a few jurors were sitting around in the courtroom at the time of my presentation. Although the judge listened quite courteously and patiently to the authorities I had to present, he very quickly overruled them. Some of the jurors in the courtroom pretty well got the drift of the contentions and while I did not hope to get my point sustained, I wanted to save it for an appeal to the Oklahoma Criminal Court of Appeals and finally to the Supreme Court of the United States should that be necessary. I think I derived some advantage from presenting it. In a town the size of Durant, Oklahoma, things spread fast, and I think the townspeople got the theory of the defense quite well.

Pete's stepfather, Frank Hessbrook, engaged another young lawyer in Durant for help in picking the jury. His name was Alan McPheron, and I left the selection of the jury largely to him and Mr. Steger. I think they did a very fine job, and we had as good a jury as we could have possibly picked for a case of that type.

The presentation of the prosecution's case was necessarily rather brief. They put on several officers who described how they had tracked Traxler trying to arrest him, detailing his numerous escapes from the net they'd drawn and finally, recounting his surrender after a gun battle about 20 miles outside Durant. They also testified that they had recovered Trimmer's car out in that area. Mr. Trimmer and his wife were both placed on the stand where they described Traxler's drawing a shotgun on them and demanding that they surrender their automobile to him and how he fled in the car. I tried to develop from Trimmer Traxler's personal appearance, showing that he had not shaved in a couple of weeks and appeared to be drawn and hungry and probably weakened in his bodily movements. All of this was calculated to demonstrate Traxler's desperate anxiety to escape.

Once the State had introduced its evidence and rested its

case, all eyes turned to me. Everyone seemed to be wondering what I would do. Most of the spectators and court attaches were astounded when I asked Roy Pete Traxler to take the stand.

The district attorney had become very kindly disposed toward me and asked the Court to excuse him for a whispered conference with me. He said, "I like to show every courtesy I can to a visiting lawyer, and I really don't believe you know the record of this fellow or you wouldn't put him on the stand. I have here his prison record listing how many times he has been convicted and of what crimes and the different penitentiaries he has served in, and I'll be glad to let you have it and examine it if you want to before you have him testify. Of course, if you insist on having him testify, it will be my duty to drag all of these other convictions in to let the jury know just what kind of man you are asking them to believe."

I thanked him and told him that I was aware of Traxler's criminal record and had decided to go that route and take my chances on the effect it would have.

Traxler made a splendid witness for himself. He was frank and truthful about every incident, and there wasn't much left for him to be browbeaten about on cross-examination. I brought out from him that he had been born and reared in Oklahoma and had come up under a stepfather, that he had never seen his father and did not know at that time whether he was living or dead, and that his stepfather had been very cruel to him and had driven him away from home—after which Traxler began his career of crime. He detailed every house of detention, penitentiary, and jail where he had been held and all of the charges against him but solemnly said that he had never taken a human life. He told about the robbery in Lipscomb County and how he was sent from there to the Huntsville penitentiary. Traxler related being put down on the Eastham Farm to work in the cotton fields—although he was frail in body and could not stand the heat—and how his wife, Nell Traxler—knowing his condition—smuggled in the guns with which he made his escape. He detailed all the rounds and escapes he had in Oklahoma and his various battles with the law officers. Traxler described how, although he was physically exhausted, he was still continuing his efforts to escape when the car he was driving ran out of gas and how, knowing the officers were close behind him and would overtake him if he didn't get another car, he—with a gun—took the car of Mr. and Mrs. Trimmer.

It all made quite a dramatic story. I said, "Now, Pete, would you tell this jury what your intentions were when you took Mr. Trimmer's car? In other words, did you take that car for the purpose of appropriating it to your own use and benefit and making it your property, or did you take it for the purpose of effecting your escape from the officers?"

He answered, "Mr. Bracewell, I never had any other thought when I took that car than to drive it until it gave out of gas and then leave it on the road for Mr. Trimmer to recover."

"Do you tell the jury now that you had no thought of stealing Mr. Trimmer's car?"

"I must solemnly say I never had that thought."

"Now, Pete, this record shows that you were put in the penitentiary and after serving several months effected your escape and were later tried at Huntsville and acquitted of robbery in this case. Tell the jury whether or not you have ever had any trouble of any kind or character since that time."

"Sir, I have not."

"Have you obeyed every rule, regulation, and law of the State of Texas and the penitentiary authorities at Huntsville, so far as you know?"

"I have."

"The record shows that you regained your freedom in about 1943. What did you do at that time?"

"I went to work for a construction company near Huntsville."

"How long did you work for them?"

"I worked for them five or six months until they moved to Denton, Texas."

"State whether or not you violated any law or regulation during the time you worked for this construction company."

"I did not."

"Now, I believe you were arrested there and taken to Oklahoma to answer for the offense which you are being tried on here."

"Yes, sir."

"Did you make bond and obtain your release from the jail there in Durant after you were arrested and got back to Oklahoma?"

"Yes, sir."

"Who made your bond?"

"Mr. Alton Jones, one of the businessmen here in Durant."

"Now, where did you go from here after you obtained your release?"

"I went to Wharton, Texas, and became employed by a plumbing concern."

"Who is the sheriff of Wharton County?"

"Buckshot Lane."

"Did you report to Mr. Lane and tell him all about your record and the prison sentence that you had had, etc.?"

"Yes, sir, I did."

"Have you continuously worked for that firm in Wharton since your release, and are you now employed by that firm?"

"Yes, sir."

"If this jury should acquit you, are you willing and do you promise to be a peaceful, law-abiding citizen from here on out?"

"Yes, sir."

Such was substantially the testimony Traxler gave at his trial. This was reinforced by the deposition of several prominent people, including Sheriff Lane, who had known him and had observed his conduct in Wharton. They all said that Traxler had pursued a course of exemplary conduct.

At about this juncture, the everfaithful E. R. Wright arrived on a bus, having traveled all night for the purpose of testifying. I put him on the stand, and he detailed the incidents of the trial at Huntsville and the promise which he and I made Traxler at the time of his acquittal. Mr. Wright described how he had assisted Traxler in getting a job after he had finally been released in Texas. He added that he had followed Traxler's conduct very closely since that time and was familiar with every phase of it.

"Now, Mr. Wright," I said, "based upon all your experience with R. P. Traxler and his career of crime—as well as his course of conduct since his acquittal in Huntsville of the charge of robbery by firearms as has been detailed in this court—state whether or not in your judgment he is a man of honor and integrity and will tell the truth on all occasions."

"Absolutely."

"Do you believe his testimony under oath given in a court of justice?"

"Yes, sir."

This, in brief, was our testimony at the trial in Durant. The court charged the jury upon the law of robbery and also affirmatively charged them on the law of temporary taking, to the effect that unless they believed beyond a reasonable doubt that Traxler took Trimmer's car for the purpose of appropriating it for his own use and benefit, they should acquit him. A short time later, both sides had completed their arguments. These were similar to those that might be heard in any criminal case of this character. The district attorney stressed the brazen nature of the holdup and the great wrong and indignity that had been done Mr. and Mrs. Trimmer by taking their car. I, of course, stressed the proposition that Traxler had served ten years in Huntsville under an illegal sentence and that he had won the admiration of all the prison officials and of the townspeople of Wharton and that his reformation was such that he was entitled to sympathetic consideration. I reminded the jury that Traxler had said that he had not intended to take the automobile for the purpose of stealing it and that they were bound to take such testimony as being true in view of all the corroborating circumstances and the testimony as to his good conduct and his reputation for truth and veracity in Wharton.

The jury had been retired for about two hours when reports began to pour in about the terrible blowup of a ship loaded with high explosives in the harbor at Texas City. It was one of the most devastating tragedies that had happened in the United States in a century. Texas City was close to Houston, and I had many friends living there—and relatives as well. I made the facts known to the Court and to opposing counsel, and they all agreed that I should immediately leave for Houston and Texas City.

The next day Mr. McPheron phoned me in Houston to say that the jury was hopelessly deadlocked. They had deliberated for over 30 hours. He seemed to have a way of finding out how the jury stood, and he told me that his best information was that the jurors were seven for acquittal and five for conviction. I told him that if he did not think there was any hope of agreement and acquittal, he should ask that the jury be discharged. I reached this conclusion a little more readily because I felt sure that if a majority of the jurors were for acquittal, the State of Oklahoma would never try the case again and that would be tantamount to an acquittal. After keeping the jurors together for another half day, Judge Sullivan dismissed them and entered a mistrial.

Pete went back to Wharton and resumed his employment as a plumber. His employer had a lot of work in Palacios, which was adjacent to Wharton. Months and months went by without a move to set the case for another trial. Then came a political campaign during which the matter was rehashed and the candidates who eventually won pledged to retry the case and put Pete Traxler in the penitentiary. So after about another year, the case was set for trial again, and I returned to Durant, where I had somewhat the same experiences as I had during the first trial. Although the testimony was about the same, the Court and the district attorney had decided that they would not charge the jury on the issue of temporary taking. That cut the ground out from under my best argument for an acquittal. The judge merely charged the jury on taking with a felonious intent, which to most people means an unlawful intent. Of course, this ruled out my main contention. At any rate, after a strenuous trial, the jury stayed out for a long time and finally came in with a minimum sentence of five years in the penitentiary.

Many of the jurors were deeply moved by the story Traxler revealed to them and said with tears that they felt impelled to impose penitentiary sentence. Over half the jurors agreed to immediately sign an application to the governor for a pardon and thereby obtain Traxler's release in a manner which was thoroughly consistent with their oath as jurors.

I returned to Houston with a heavy heart because I had been

thoroughly convinced of the righteousness of my cause, yet had not prevailed. I felt that if the judge had given the charge on temporary taking as he had the first time, I would have unquestionably obtained an acquittal. The road of appeal to the Court of Criminal Appeals in Oklahoma City was left open, of course. It was 1951, and I had now fought the case 13 years. It looked as if there would be no end to it. But I made up my mind that I would see it through to the finish by appealing it.

An appeal is a slow process. It took two or three months to get up the record. In the meantime, Pete was released on bond and went back to his job in Palacios. The record was finally completed and the case filed, and I went to Oklahoma City to argue it. There was no question that the Oklahoma Court of Criminal Appeals had theretofore held that in robbery cases where the issue was raised, the Court had to charge the jury on temporary taking. I also had much case law to sustain my position that when a state has possession of a defendant and the means with which to try him, yet sends him off to another jurisdiction to be tried and to serve another sentence in that state, it waives the right to further try him on charges then pending in the releasing state.

The Court listened to me quite considerately, and I felt reasonably confident of my position when I left Oklahoma City. However, time passed, and the decision didn't materialize. Month after month went by, and I couldn't imagine what was holding up the opinion, unless it was that the Court was divided on the question. The decision which finally came was to the effect that while the Criminal Court of Appeals of Oklahoma had theretofore held that there must be a charge on temporary taking when the question is raised, those cases so decided were wrong and that the true rule in Oklahoma ought to be that such a charge was not necessary. They overruled the other point, which was really a federal question, and affirmed the case on December 10, 1952. [*Traxler v. State*, 96 Okla. Crim. 231, 251 P.2d 815 (Okla. Crim. App., 1952).

I decided to file a motion for rehearing. Throwing everything I had into it, I tried to persuade the Court of Appeals that it had made an error in abandoning its previous line of decisions.

On January 7, 1953, the Court filed its opinion denying that motion. No. A-11586, *Traxler v. State*, 96 Okla. Crim. 231, 251 P.2d 815 (Okla. Ct. App. 1953).

My determination to free Traxler from further imprisonment on the offenses that he had committed prior to his Huntsville trial was unabated. I investigated and found that the cost of the transcript I would need to appeal the case to the United States Supreme Court would be approximately $750. A group of citizens in Wharton had agreed to contribute money for the purpose of buying the record for this appeal when I got a letter from Traxler stating that he had thoroughly considered the matter and did not believe he would be justified in permitting his friends to put up the cost of the transcript. He said that given the sympathetic attitude of the jurors, he would probably be able to obtain a release in a few months after he went to the Oklahoma penitentiary. He added that I had represented him for so long with little or no compensation that he did not want to impose upon me further. This was the best evidence that Pete Traxler had ever produced that there was some good in him yet. I decided to abandon the appeal and let him accept the situation.

Thus ended what was probably one of the most remarkable legal contests that ever took place in this country. As he had anticipated, Pete got out after a few months and returned to Palacios to follow his trade as a plumber. He ceased to communicate with me, and after some years I inquired about him and learned that he had gone to California where he was leading an honorable life.

◆◆◆

Jury Argument in the
Case of Roy Pete Traxler
(in Durant, Oklahoma), April 16, 1947

GENTLEMEN OF THE JURY:

The life of a lawyer is not nearly so easy as some people think. There is a lot of hard work and many a heartache connected with the profession. There are, however, two compensating elements which make it to many the most alluring of all professions: one is the splendid fellowship and respect which lawyers and judges have for each other. The other is the fact that every case is so entirely different from every other case one has ever tried.

Certainly, the friendly hospitality of your judge, your county attorney and his assistant, and all the local lawyers is in keeping with the noblest traditions of the profession. I only hope that these gentlemen will some day come my way so that I may return some of the many courtesies which they have extended to me since I have been in your city engaged in the preparation and trial of this case.

The other element of professional pleasure is also abundantly present in this case—that of it being the most different and the strangest case that either judge, lawyers, or jurors have ever been privileged to participate in—different in the personality of the defendant and background of his checkered career; different in the setting and the way the offense of robbery is alleged to have been committed; different in that we are trying it practically ten years after the offense took place, and different in the fact that two states have been for this long period of time trying to punish the same defendant for what is in effect the same offense and, at least some of the time, working at cross purposes to this end.

Laws are made for the protection of society. It is so written in practically all the criminal codes that I know anything about—to protect society and reform the criminal. Vengeance does not belong to you or to me. It belongs to a Higher Authority. While you sit in the jury box as a protector of society, you have an obligation to show consideration for the unfortunate and even mercy when you consider it to be merited.

I know that you are going to perform your duties as jurors in line with what you consider your oath to be. Then why do I call your attention to these fundamental concepts of criminal law? Because 30 years in the practice of the profession has taught me what a vague and illusive thing is this matter of a "reasonable doubt" which is found in every charge on the criminal law, even as it has been ably expounded to you in this charge. It may mean almost anything. It may mean almost nothing. And jurors usually, and I think appropriately, decide a case in line with what they conceive to be their duty to society. They resolve the "reasonable doubt" to support such duty, and I am not so sure that this is not exactly as it should be.

In this case there is little or no dispute about the physical facts and those things which were done or said. Since the offense occurred nearly ten years ago, what little difference there is comes about doubtless by faulty recollection on the part of the witnesses rather than a deliberate intention to misrepresent or injure. Then why is this case particularly difficult? It is because every issue in the case as submitted to you in His Honor's charge revolves upon the question of intent on the part of the defendant. You are called upon to look into a man's heart as it existed ten years ago and base your verdict upon his intent at that time.

The crucial question is whether there was an intent to steal an automobile and appropriate it to the defendant's own use and benefit, as set forth in the charge, or whether there was an intent or escape and a mere temporary taking of the automobile with the intention of abandoning it to the owner after using it to effect such escape. There is only one person, of course, who knows for sure what that intent was, and that is Roy Pete Traxler. If you take his word for it, you will, of course, acquit him. But I make no contention that you have to take his word for it. You can disregard his testimony altogether and reach a different conclusion according to the facts and circumstances as you view them and return a verdict of guilty.

In making this argument, I propose to first review the facts and circumstances as revealed from the witness stand and show that they themselves point unerringly to a purpose of escape and temporary taking, and that in addition to this the defendant, though heretofore several times convicted as the district attorney brought forth on his cross-examination, has by a course of ten years' exemplary conduct merited having you believe his sincerity of purpose and the truthfulness of his testimony when he tells you there was no intent of appropriation.

The Court has very appropriately told you that you are entitled to draw upon your experiences in life and your knowledge of what men will do under similar circumstances [reading statements from the charge]. Let us view this alleged crime of robbery in light of the charge so ably stated by the court. The taking of this car had its inception on the 8th day of July, 1937, in the prison cotton fields of the State of Texas in the Trinity River bottom. No man can understand the conditions existing there at that time without having been there. It may appropriately be termed the "Alcatraz of Texas." The heat was terrible, and these prisoners were working under the gun. They longed for their freedom. They wanted it more than anything else in the world. They were willing to take a chance to gain it. There were 15 of them, including the defendant and Fred Tindol. Is there a man on the jury who for one moment thinks that any of them, including the defendant, entertained a thought of theft and permanent appropriation of property at that time? To suggest such a purpose is almost absurd.

They made the wild break, and the first thing they did was to relieve two officers of their guns, out of which the two Walker County indictments grew. Why did they take the guns? Was it for the purpose of theft or for the purpose of escape? Twelve jurors of Walker County, acting within a very short time after the occurrence when everything was fresh in the minds of the witnesses, held that the purpose was escape and not theft—but a further discussion of these trials a little later on.

Now, what did these defendants do between the 8th day of July, 1937, and nine days later when they took Frank Trimmer's car? The testimony shows that there was a wild flight in an effort to gain freedom and that they were at times pursued by what some estimated to be a thousand officers.

One witness said that he saw as many as 20 carloads pursuing the defendant at one time. The defendant and Tindol took automobiles as they came to them. They ran one until it gave out of gas, abandoned it to the owner, and took another car. The defendant says that he does not know how many cars they took in this manner. But they abandoned them and left them all to the owners as soon as the gas gave out. They finally came to the car belonging to Jim Denton, who has testified as a witness before you. And this man Denton seems to me to be the very salt of the earth. He does not want to do any man any wrong. They took Denton and forced him to go with them. Did they intend to steal Denton's car? Denton tells you that so far as he could determine, there was no other thought on the part of anybody except to drive the car until it gave out of gas and then leave it to be recovered by the owner. That is exactly what happened. They did so abandon Denton's car near the home of Frank Trimmer.

This brings us to the identical charge laid in the indictment. I doubt if anyone could say that the two had the slightest intent of stealing anybody else's car besides Trimmer's. Now, what happened at Trimmer's house? He and his wife were preparing to get in the car—Trimmer having the intention of driving his wife to the school where she was teaching. Traxler and Tindol first said that they wanted to buy some gas, and Trimmer told them that he had only two gallons in his car. This is verified by his wife. When he found out they were going to take his car, he told them that it wouldn't go far because it was in bad repair and the knee-action was broken. Trimmer admits that he knew, or at least thought, they were escaping convicts. This indicates that he did not think they were going to permanently appropriate his car. In the conversation that followed, Mrs. Trimmer got virtually the same idea. She wanted them to leave her husband and said something to the effect that they could drive the car as far as they wanted to and leave it. When the Trimmers were pressed on the witness stand for any facts or circumstances that would lead them to think that there was any intent to permanently appropriate the car, they both gave none.

Under such circumstances, they left the Trimmer home

with Traxler driving the car. Trimmer was on the front seat with him, and Denton and Tindol were on the rear seat. After going a certain distance, when doubtless the two gallons were almost exhausted, they got to Cade's filling station. Under Trimmer's testimony, the tank at that time would have held more than 12 gallons of gas. And right here, gentlemen of the jury, is a fact that to my mind absolutely refutes any intent of permanent appropriation. Trimmer tells you, as Traxler tells you, that Traxler only had five gallons of gas put in the car. Before any man on this jury votes for a conviction based upon an intent of permanently appropriating the car, let him ask and answer to his own conscience the question of why Traxler bought only five gallons of gas. Traxler tells you that he intended to drive the car to the point where they ultimately stopped and leave Trimmer enough gas to get back home on. Certainly this was reasonable, and to say that he intended to keep the car when he had the money for the full 12 gallons in his pocket and only got five gallons of gas, although he was pursued by a thousand officers, is a ridiculous proposition.

From there they went to the scene of the shooting and the death of Tindol. They stopped the car by the roadside, and there is a wide disparity between what Denton and Trimmer think happened at that time. Denton says that Tindol and Traxler fell asleep and that Denton wrestled their guns from them and shot them. Trimmer, making somewhat of a hero of himself, says he struggled for Traxler's gun, took it way from him, and shot him. This is not important, because Denton and Trimmer had the right to shoot them whether they were asleep or awake, but it is highly important in terms of Mr. Trimmer's recollection as to what happened. These men had been on the run for eight days. They had not shaved; they were dirty; they were bleary-eyed—according to Mr. Denton and Traxler. When the car stopped, they fell asleep. This is important in that it shows that the men were even incapable from a physical standpoint of entertaining a criminal intent.

So, from all the facts as they occurred from the time of the flight from the Eastham Farm on the Trinity River to the shooting of Traxler by the roadside, as detailed by the witnesses, everything goes to refute an intent of theft. There is not a man in the courtroom who could think that the charge would ever have been filed or seriously pressed were it not for the fact that Pete Traxler, the defendant—due to the errors of his youth—has served four terms in the penitentiary and happens to be the defendant on trial. And this brings us to the next phase of the case: the question of whether or not Traxler—with his record—is worthy of belief at the hands of this jury.

There is a challenge in this phase of the case. The assistant county attorney would have you believe that because of previous convictions, Traxler is unworthy of belief. This in a measure puts you and me—all organized society—on trial. It puts to a test a lot of our boasted professions. We teach that "as long as the taper burns, the vilest sinner may return." We urge reformation and repentance. We do a lot to restore fallen men and women to an honorable place in society. Yet in this case when you have ten years of exemplary conduct on the part of the defendant under the most adverse circumstances under which a human being could live, you have the State—through its prosecuting official—telling you that even though he has reformed, he is still unworthy of belief and that he must continue to live under the suspicion of a felon. If we, and you the jury, are to say by our conduct that this man must remain so branded as long as he lives, I don't see how we could have the gall to urge reformation on the part of any wrongdoer. The minute he is sent to the penitentiary, you may as well brand him with the mark of Cain and check him off as useless rubbish in the social order. I, for one, believe that "not one life shall be destroyed and cast as rubbish to the void when the Master completes the heap" and that the deeper a man sinks in depravity, the more marvelous and complete regeneration and restoration may be.

The evidence warrants that conclusion that the 12th day of November, 1937, was a fateful day in the life of Roy Pete Traxler. The district attorney implied that he probably was not vigorously prosecuted in Huntsville due to the fact that my brother was district attorney and I was on the defense counsel, but the facts show that if there ever was a man prosecuted with all the power that the State could bring to bear, Pete Traxler was so prosecuted at that trial. We had not only a district attorney and an able county attorney, such as you have here, but they were reinforced with the skill of a state senator and still further by what the evidence shows to be one of the greatest lawyers of East Texas, employed especially by the governor of the State of Texas. Traxler already had a life sentence. Why this high-powered prosecution? There is only one answer. The State took the position that Pete Traxler had forfeited every right to live, and their sole purpose was to obtain the death penalty.

With the most resourceful prosecution that the State could afford, it would seem that the hand of Providence was laid upon Traxler when the jury of Walker County—on that memorable day—handed in a verdict of not guilty, thereby refuting the robbery motive in his taking guns on the same flight as this car was taken. Something happened to Pete Traxler at that time. The evidence shows that he resolved that he was going to lead the life of a law-abiding convict and citizen from that day on and salvage whatever might be left of a life which—to that time—had been worthless. So far as this record goes, he has scrupulously kept that high resolve from that day until this. Are you to reward his efforts at this time by the imposition of another penitentiary sentence?

The record is almost silent on the seven long years intervening, but in December, 1944, fate again took a turn at Fortune's wheel when the Court of Criminal Appeals of the State of Texas held that Traxler's conviction was void and he had been illegally detained in the Texas State Penitentiary during all of that time. The Court, however, ordered him to Lipscomb County to stand trial on the original indictment. Did Lipscomb County send for him? No! He was transferred to Fayette County to stand trial on the remaining Walker County indictment, which had been transferred there. A long wait ensued in Fayette County and then for another six months in Walker County. All this time, he was ready and demanding a trial, and yet the State did not bring him to trial. Finally, an inquiry was made to the Oklahoma authorities as to what they expected to do. They said they would not seek to obtain him until Texas got through. Thereupon, E. R. Wright, that eminent citizen of the City of Huntsville who has testified before you, sought and obtained Traxler's bond—and he walked forth, a free man for the first time in nine years.

What was his conduct subsequent to that time? He obtained a responsible position; worked on the college campus; lived openly at the hotel for a period of four months—making good on a resolve to rebuild a misspent life. He was then transferred to Denton County to pursue the same employment with the same employer and make a living wage. And finally, six months after his release, the State of Oklahoma—for some unexplained reason—decided that it would again issue a warrant for his arrest and bring him back to stand trial on this old indictment filed in 1937.

I do not criticize your local officers. They say they wanted to try him ten years ago when the offense was first committed, but that some undisclosed power in Oklahoma City prevailed upon the governor of Oklahoma to deny to them their right—and Traxler's right—of a speedy trial and directed them to convey him to the State of Texas to resume the service of what they thought was a life sentence. So far as this record discloses, neither your local officers nor Frank Trimmer have been eager to press this prosecution, and a big question mark has arisen as to where this prosecution stems from. Is it possible that vague, undisclosed power of Oklahoma City has again prevailed upon the governor to dispatch his law enforcement officers and forcibly return Traxler to the State of Oklahoma to stand trial at this late date on a charge which was pending at a time when they forcibly extradited him from the state?

I know that you want to be just. We do not ask for mercy, as stated by the county attorney, but we ask for justice. This man has done great wrongs, of course, but that he has already suffered equally great punishment is hardly open to question. I have a feeling that tomorrow evening an aged mother will sit down with her son, from whom she has been separated for more than ten years, and they will break bread in an humble home in Rush Springs, Oklahoma. And as they break bread, they will lift their voices in thanks to Him who guides all human destinies, and as they give thanks, they will ask His richest blessings upon the jury which gave Roy Pete Traxler his freedom.

◆◆◆

Romance of a Light Bill

ONE OF THE interesting families which was playing a substantial part in the development of Houston when I went there to practice law in 1916 was the Scanlan "Daughters." I use the word "daughters" instead of "sisters" in deference to what appeared to me to be an overly-sensitive feeling on their part about the use of the word "sisters." There were four of them named—in the order of their ages—as follows: Frances, Kate, Lillian and Stella. None ever married. Their father was one of the early mayors of Houston serving in carpet-bag days, which probably enhanced their unpopularity. They built quite a large mansion at the corner of Gray Avenue and Main Street, which is now in downtown Houston. After the father's death, the daughters continued to occupy the mansion—living almost absolutely in seclusion. The fact that they were of the Catholic faith rather encouraged newspaper reporters in all publicity about them to refer to them as the Scanlan "sisters." They deeply resented it, but were without any power on earth to counteract it. As much as their intimates could do to spread the knowledge among newspaper people and reporters that they resented the terms "sisters," it seemed the more the journalistic fraternity would refer to them in those terms.

The elder Scanlans acquired an estate of several million dollars before they died. Much of it was invested in real estate in the City of Houston and large acreage tracts in the vicinity of the towns of Humble and Arcola, both in Harris County. In addition to this, they undoubtedly owned a large amount of liquid assets stashed away in several banks and investment companies of the north and east because very few people, if any, ever learned the nature of their assets.

They left no will. It was widely reported and believed that the pair left a will in which it was provided that they should share the property equally and that the oldest living sister should manage the property, and if either should ever marry, she would forfeit all of her interest in the estate. If such a will ever existed, it was never probated and I don't think it ever existed.

But by common agreement among themselves, the oldest of the four daughters would act as manager of the estate with as absolute authority as any owner ever exercised over his individual property. They never sold any land and, as a consequence, it was never necessary for all of them to participate in signing deeds in order to convey title.

One tract they owned was at the corner of Main and Preston—the site of the White House of Texas and at that time—that is about the year 1917—was at the very hub of the downtown area of Houston. They conceived the idea, during Miss Francis' lifetime, of building the largest and most modern building in the city of Houston on that corner, and they had the liquid assets with which to do it without borrowing any money. It was a beautiful 12-story building and at that time, the privilege of officing in such a building was at quite a premium. It, likewise, housed one of the newer and more modern banks of the city. About the time the building was completed and ready for operation, Miss Frances died and, of course, Miss Kate was next in line of succession to the management of the vast estate. She, at that time, was probably 65 years old.

Miss Kate soon became known among lawyers and public officials as a person who would fight at the drop of a hat about anything and was as stubborn as a mule. A person handling an estate of that size will naturally have some litigation, and she became widely known as a person who could, with the greatest dexterity, dodge the service of process by the officers. She kept them locked out—without admittance—while they would stay waiting for hours for her to come out so they would serve her with process. She had private escape hatches from the building and always eluded them. They tried time and again to serve her while she was getting in her carriage to leave the building and tried various ruses to get in the house and serve her at home. She could leave the building from the basement. Her regular attorney was Walter Brown, a very able lawyer who had a reputation of being about as resourceful as she was. He refused to take part in many of her little controversies and managed to be out of the city, and I became one of her substitute lawyers.

I shall never forget one time she summoned me to her office when she was almost in a frenzy and wanted me to get out an injunction against the City of Houston. On the development of the facts, it occurred that the City of Houston was putting in a curb and gutter street that was beside one of her pieces of property and was actually encroaching on her land 4 inches. Of course, I managed to sidestep it till Mr. Brown got back and the suit was never filed.

Once she recovered a judgment against Foley Bros. for $75,000 for damages to her partition wall separating. The case was carried all the way to the Supreme Court, but Miss Kate won the long and bitter controversy. The lawyer for Foley's insurance carrier finally—in great humility—carried the check for the entire amount calculated to the last penny and laid it on Miss Kate's desk before her.

Miss Kate drew herself up with great dignity and scorn and said, "No I will not receive the check in payment. My judgment calls for payment in money, and I insist on being paid that way." After several frantic telephone calls to New York and Chicago, the lawyer brought in 75 one-thousand-dollar bills, and the odd dollars and cents, her opponents thereby draining the cup to its bitterest dregs.

These things all had wide publicity and the public got an entirely distorted view of Miss Kate. She was, to her friends at least, a kindly person who was given to charity and was never known to fail anybody in a time of need. So was Miss Lillian. Their unannounced deeds of charity would fill a large volume.

About 1927, I moved to the Scanlan Building. At that time, many other large office buildings had been constructed further south on Main Street and it was not difficult to get into the

Scanlan Building. In fact, at the time I moved in, there was considerable vacant space in it. The First National Bank Building had been enlarged, the Union National Bank Building had been built, the Esperson Building, the West Building, the Second National Bank Building, and others that might be mentioned, all of which had come to be regarded as more desirable as an office building than The Scanlan Building.

In the meantime, I had been President of the controversial Taxpayers' Association for several years and, having been tax attorney for Harris County, I was regarded by many people as a capable tax lawyer. The City and County had fixed the tax valuation on the Scanlan Building while it was the hub of the city, and as these other buildings were constructed further south and the city grew that way, it was obvious that the Scanlan Building had become less and less valuable. The city was wedded to the front-foot method of valuation, plus the replacement cost of the improvements on the property, and that method was entirely erroneous as applied to that building with the attendant trend in city growth.

Miss Kate employed me to try to get her evaluations down to a point commensurate with the actual yield of the building. This began a 10-year controversy before we finally received a satisfactory adjustment and reduction of the taxes, both of which had accumulated during the years and also that which was to accumulate in the future.

This has been a long prelude to the story of the light bill, but it seemed to be necessary for a proper understanding of the controversy to understand the forces and personalities behind it. As the depression wore on, the Scanlan Building became about 50% empty. The Light Company gauged the price per kilowatt hour on the number of openings in the establishment—the more openings, the greater the rate. The way it was set up, the consumer had to pay for all the openings even in that part of the building which was not being occupied, had not been occupied for several years, and which there was no hope of it being occupied in a reasonable time in the future. The light bill had accumulated to $5,000 or $6,000 without Miss Kate ever having said very much about it. The estate being an extremely wealthy one, the Light Company did not push it as they might have a smaller consumer. From a legal standpoint, it looked like "a long shot" and Mr. Brown did not want to have anything to do with it.

Miss Kate applied to me to try to get some relief. The Light Company had told her that if the accumulated bill was not paid within a certain time, they were going to cut the lights off for the entire building, tenants and all. She wanted me to get an injunction against The Light Company from cutting off her service. Contrary to the generally-accepted idea, a lawyer just cannot go to the courthouse and pull an injunction out of the hat. He has to have some pretty solid basis to go on. I told Miss Kate that I frankly did not think I could get an injunction. While the method used by The Light Company in determining the rate was obviously discriminatory, the courts had not decided the question in such a way that I felt that the court would grant an injunction. Miss Kate insisted that I go in and do the best I could, and since I was considerably in arrears in my own rent and had plenty of time to attack the impossible, I decided to take a shot at it.

The case was one which was bound to attract a lot of publicity as light rates were a very touchy subject in Houston at that time. Although I was representing a large estate owned by persons who were not any too popular, still I somewhat had the underdog role in trying to do something about the discriminatory light rates in the City of Houston, from which everybody was suffering. So I filed the suit alleging that the building was half empty, due to the trend of the city growth and the construction of other large office buildings which were more modern than that of the Scanlan Building. I alleged that the kilowatt hour rate for the Scanlan Building was approximately 4¢ as against possibly 3¢ for the Union National Bank Building, 2½¢ for another comparable building and 2¢ for still another one. I was able to get this information from the building owners who were smarting under the same arbitrary rule. I alleged that the whole thing was discriminatory and she had, in fact, overpaid her bill by many thousands of dollars and asked that the Light Company be enjoined from cutting off her lights by reason of nonpayment of bill until there could be a final determination of all the questions in a jury trial. The case was set down for hearing on this application for a temporary injunction.

At the hearing, I had the burden of proof and had summoned the executive vice-president of the Light Company to attend and bring with him the record of bills of all comparable buildings. It had been rumored for a long time that the Jones Buildings had enjoyed a special rate—that is—the buildings owned by Jesse H. Jones Companies, but it seemed as if no one could ever get the facts about it. There was no question about our own rate, and all I had to do was to introduce the various statements which the Light Company had given to Miss Kate to show the rate they were actually charging her. I put the Executive Director of the Light Company on the stand and began to quiz him about what the other buildings were paying. I didn't have a lot of difficulty until I got to the Jones Buildings. I developed all of the others first because experience had taught me that when you go to tackling an empire of that size, the lawyers are sure to have a lot of technical objections, which are quite plausible. I had all of the Jones Buildings grouped together in my file and when I took them up, the first one appeared to be paying 1.09% per kilowatt hour; then the second one of the Jones Buildings appeared to be paying the same rate. I got to the third building and it appeared to be paying the same rate.

At this stage of the hearing, it was apparent that the buildings—such as the Scanlan Building, the Union National Bank Building, and the First National Bank Building and the West Building, were all paying varying rates, while the Jones Buildings were paying exactly the same rate and at a rate which was substantially lower than that which was being paid by any of the other buildings. When it became apparent that this was developing, the attorney for the Light Company began to pour in on the Trial Judge terrific objections as to the whole irrelevance and immateriality of the rates which the Jones Buildings were paying because the Executive Director of the Light Company admitted that they were on a special arrangement, and an arrangement which was not applicable to the other buildings. There was, of course, some reason for the objection and I did not argue a very long time until the Judge was shutting off all further testimony about the Jones Buildings because they were on a different rate by private contract and did not come under the regular-scheduled rate published by the company.

Since there was not much else to do in the light of this ruling, the Trial Court refused the temporary injunction which, of course, left the Light Company free to cut off all service to the entire building, and if that had been done, the Scanlan estate would have been subjected to numerous well-founded lawsuits by the tenants for not having paid the bill and kept up the service. I very promptly gave notice of appeal to the Court of Civil Appeals at Galveston. But under the rules, of course, the injunction was not in force and the Light Company might have cut off the lights should they have elected to do so.

On the other hand, the Light Company had developed certain hazards which it would run should it cut off the lights. If, upon a final hearing before a jury, it was found that the light bills were in point discriminatory and she had paid far more than her light bills would have amounted to under the rates that the Jones Buildings were paying, the Light Company would have been subjected to a tremendous lawsuit by the Scanlan Estate and very probably by some of the tenants of the Scanlan Estate.

Miss Kate directed me to go ahead and appeal the case as quickly as I could. Immediately, I filed the cost bond and ordered the transcript of the proceedings which, of course, takes several days and sometimes weeks to prepare and sat back to see whether or not the Light Company would, in fact, cut the lights off in the building. I was not much surprised and, of course, considerably elated when they did not cut the lights off. I went ahead preparing the appeal and since such cases have a preference on the docket of the Appellate Court and it was not but about 60 days before we had the hearing in the Appellate Court.

As the case progressed, I became more and more confident of the law which was involved, but on the other hand, the matter of granting or refusing a temporary injunction is always almost entirely in the discretion of the Trial Court, and there was not much hope of getting the Appellate Court to hold that the Trial Court had abused its discretion in refusing the injunction.

There was a large merchandise hatch on the north side of the Scanlan Building, which I walked over every morning in going to my office. In this interim, on many occasions, I would be going to the office and I noticed various quantities of material and parts of machinery being let down through this hatch into the basement of the Scanlan Building. However, I did not pay a lot of attention to it. It was nothing unusual about a building of that kind.

When the case was heard in the Court of Appeals in Galveston, the Court was quite interested in all my theories of the case and the law involved, but I ran into the very rule I had anticipated to the effect that the Trial Judge did not abuse his discretion in refusing the injunction. After two or three weeks, the court rendered its decision upholding the trial court in refusing the injunction. I was very much discouraged by this time, but Miss Kate couldn't take defeat and she wanted to press on relentlessly to the Supreme Court. Under our rules, the Supreme Court has 30 days in which you can make an application for a writ of error—if they think the law questions involved are substantial, they grant the writ and review the whole case.

At Miss Kate's insistence, I applied to the Supreme Court for a writ of error, noticing that the activity through the sidewalk hatch continued all this time, presumably getting ready for the winter months. Finally, after about another six weeks, the Supreme Court notified us that they refused the application for a writ of error and, of course, we were at our row's end.

After the mandate got back from the Supreme Court, the Light Company very promptly notified Miss Kate that they were going to cut off the lights if the bill was not paid in so many hours. Miss Kate ignored the notice and the Light Company, true to their threat, proceeded to disconnect the entire light system from the Scanlan building.

But to their utter amazement and chagrin, nothing

happened. The lighting of the building continued right on as if nothing had happened. Upon investigation, they discovered that Miss Kate had, while the case was on appeal, constructed her own entirely new light plant in the basement of her building at a cost of $15,000 or $20,000 and, in effect, thumbed her nose at the Light Company.

The Light Company then was put to the necessity of going ahead and trying its case on the light bills and obtaining an ordinary judgment and collecting the bill on execution, the same as any other debt. They threatened around awhile and got the case set as if they were going to proceed to judgment, but I had a feeling all along that they were not anxious to try the case. It was not too long that they began to make overtures of settlement, and we settled the bill, which at that time totaled $7,000 or $8,000 for a very small percentage of the total amount.

As a sequel, it may be said that Miss Kate found the operation of her private light plant very expensive and grossly out of proportion to what her light bills would have been had she paid the discriminatory rate demanded by The Light Company. After about three years, she made her peace with The Light Company and junked her light plant. So far as I know, they have been satisfactory customers of The Light Company ever since.

At this writing, all of the Scanlan daughters have died and it is my understanding that all the property—almost intact— was left to the Catholic Church.

◆◆◆

Tribute to the Parker Brothers

THOSE OF US who have been privileged to spend most of our lives in Harrisburg have been blessed in many ways. It is not only the richest area in the State—and possibly in the nation— in its boundless possibilities for commerce and industry, but most of all in the richness of its traditions. Many of the great families of Texas have lived here, made their fortunes here, and left their wholesome and benevolent influence for the guidance of future generations.

We could begin the long list with the family of the Harisses, founders of Harris County and Harrisburg. Then follow with Revolutionary heroes such as David G. Burnett and Thomas J. Rusk and finally, the families of John G. Tod, C. H. Milby, George Hammac, James S. Deady, Tobe Collins, John Milby and many others.

Now we are to add to that galaxy that of William R. or Captain Bill Parker. It may be that because we were closer to him in point of time, or because those of us living now loved him more, but somehow we are constrained to utter: "Surely he was the noblest Roman of them all."

Born within a stone's throw of Harrisburg—at the mouth of Greens Bayou—he became a child of nature, and by most standards would have been termed a diamond in the rough. He was destined to become a pendulum, an hour glass and a social compass in a vast area joining the forces of Caption W. D. Haden, the pioneer shell producer. He soon acquired most of the art of handling floating equipment. He became known as the unerring pilot of the Houston Ship Channel and Galveston Bay.

The pilots, mates and dockhands that plied Buffalo Bayou in the early days constituted a sturdy lot as they would congregate at Uncle Joe Buckner's Saloon in old Harrisburg. It was near the docks where the innumerable small craft would tie up. Captain Bill, though a non-drinker, had that magnetic personal attraction that gained their love and affection. Little did they realize that there stood among them one who was destined to become a master pilot in the affairs of men.

How he and his four hardly less-remarkable brothers, Charley, Bob, George and Briscoe—all pilots—decided to go into the oyster shell business with no resources or equipment, has become familiar history in Houston and the surrounding area. It is a fact worthy of note that they seemed to turn instinctively to Captain Bill, second in point of age, as their leader. Probably their astute—though deeply-consecrated— Mother had a hand in his selection. At any rate, it would seem to have been by divine direction that he was selected.

It is a great tribute to the four brothers that they followed his leadership unwaveringly through one of the most amazing careers of "empire building" in the annals of Texas. The same may be said of all his department heads and employees. They relied implicitly in the wisdom of all his plans. He was kindly and considerate toward all of their problems. They became aware that he was absolutely devoid of all selfishness. As a result, he ruled through love and admiration. His every wish became a rule of action. The only argument was "What does Captain Bill want?"

While the whole State of Texas will ever owe a debt of gratitude to Captain W. D. Haden for his pioneering work in the oyster-shell industry, it was destined to make its greatest advances through his pupils—the Parker Brothers—led by Captain Bill. Mud shell for surfacing was its first great use. The mud had adhesive quality which greatly facilitated its use. The Parkers saw that the mud was a great hindrance in its use for other purposes induced for its lime content. Through them developed the great process of washing the shell through screens at the dredge side, letting the mud back into the sea. This made possible its use for lime, fertilizer, chicken feed, cement, magnesium, paper, etc.

Then came the great process of coating shell particles with asphalt at the plant, so it could be transported cold and in bulk to the jobsite. There it could be rolled out and tamped, becoming a hard-paved surface—without the old heating and mixing process.

And finally came the process of separating the fine shell from the coarse shell in the washing process. There could be no purpose in making great expenditures in crushing oyster shell into fine particles before use when the fine particles could be salvaged from the ocean bed and used without crushing. The beneficial results from this process are incalculable. Captain Bill probably regarded this as his greatest achievement.

In becoming the world's leader in oyster shell production, three operating companies were established, viz., Parker Brothers and Company, Inc., in Houston, the Matagorda Shell Company at Matagorda, and the Lake Charles Dredging Company at Lafayette, Louisiana.

They foresaw the great possibilities involved in the ready-mixed concrete business, particularly in a rapidly-growing world city such as Houston. While they had almost come to believe anything could be done—and done better with oyster shell—they recognized that most engineers would specify gravel aggregate instead of shell aggregate for concrete. They moved resolutely to meet this situation and acquired large deposits of gravel and were soon in the gravel business in a big way.

In doing all this, they built up quite a fleet of floating equipment, such as dredges, tugs, barges and small transportation boats. It was quite expensive to keep it all in repair, and besides, there was no place then to get it done and done expeditiously. This lead to the decision to establish a shipyard near the mouth of Green's Bayou. It has grown to be a quite sizable institution caring for their needs, but also the needs of many other people in a similar business.

The shipyard was the key that unlocked the doors of many opportunities; they built large oil barges and soon saw the opportunity for service and profits in water transportation. This lead to the acquiring of the Sioux City Barge Line and now their boats ply not only the intercoastal canal, but the Mississippi, Missouri, Ohio and other rivers.

Their local operations have required the development of a larger motor transportation system and also a distribution company familiarly known as the South End Building Material Company, also the acquiring of the John Young Company, primarily for the distribution of Oyster Shell; the Matagorada Shell Company was organized and now is a large dredging company under the direction of Captain Bob Parker; large shell deposits were acquired in Louisiana and the Lake Charles Dredging Company is one of the major companies developed under Captain Bill's leadership.

In these vast enterprises of oyster shell, gravel, ready-mixed concrete for building and water transportation, it is unbelievable how few controversies appeared in court and practically all of them were settled before they came to the stage of a court trial. Captain Bill was always so generous in his concessions that—in practically every instance—his adversaries became his friends.

In this era of vast industrialization and government regulation, they were thrown into contact with numerous regulatory bodies, both state and federal. Among these may be mentioned the Commissioners' Court and City Council, the Game, Fish and Oyster Commissions of Texas and Louisiana, the Railroad Commission of Texas, the Interstate Commerce Commission, the Wage and Hour Board, the Labor Board, the Internal Revenue Department, and the Corps of Engineers for the War Department. Upon my professional honor I can say that—though we lost many of our contentions—in each instance, Captain Bill came away with increased respect and admiration from the government officials.

Few employers of labor ever had employees more devoted to him than did Captain Bill. Though the number grew to nearly 1,000, he established and maintained a personal touch with them. He shared their sorrows—as well as their joys—and went to their rescue in time of trouble. Early in his career, he was deceived by a labor union and became resolutely opposed to the unionization of his operations. Through the interest and loyalty of the employees, various picketing of the teamsters to force recognition never succeeded. Notwithstanding this, he retained the admiration and respect of most of the responsible union leaders of this area.

He took a deep interest in politics. He recognized that few people who run for public office are financially able to do so and always contributed liberally to the support of his favorites. Those who knew him well will agree that he never expected an official to do other than his sworn duty after he was elected. When they came to recognize the sincerity of his motives, they listened to him with the greatest consideration.

Being children of adversity, the Parker Brothers have been overresponsive to the needs of the unfortunate. Their charities and benevolences were far flung, though seldom known to the general public. The establishment of the Milby Memorial Methodist and our own Broadway School had their most liberal support. They were believers of sports and wholesome recreation, and these activities will bear traces of their generous support and influence.

Such is a brief outline of a saga of success that has few parallels in the history of America's free enterprise system. It is one of the ironies of life; it came to an abrupt end March 21, 1962, through an instrumentality of their great achievement. They had gone to Kansas in their private plane to attend the funeral of a friend and official of the Sioux Company. The plane was piloted by a son-in-law, Glen Draper—and from causes which must forever remain unknown—he, Captain Bill, Captain Briscoe and Jack, Captain Bill's younger son, were dashed into eternity. The tragedy occurred on a lonely mountain top in Eastern Arkansas with only angels to minister and make record of the heroism with which they died.

Captain Bill often said that Captain Briscoe was the greatest pilot he had ever known. But pilots they were, one and all. Not only upon the water and in the air, but pilots upon the sea of human affairs—turbulent by the ebb and flow of the angry tides of the most revolutionary period of human history.

The overwhelming shock and grief of their friends and loved ones must be assuaged by the lines of the poet:

When from out of the bourne of time and place
the tide shall carry me far.
I hope to meet my Pilot face to face
when I have crossed the Bar.

◆◆◆

Appendix 2

Selected Writings of J. S. Bracewell

"The Lawyer"

*Address delivered before the graduates of the
Houston Law School at Sidney Lanier School,
June 1, 1939)*

MR. PRESIDENT, MEMBERS OF THE CLASS OF 1939,
LADIES AND GENTLEMEN:

I am indeed grateful for the privilege of delivering this
address to you upon an occasion which means so much in your
professional lives. You have honored me far beyond my dessert
as a lawyer. The consciousness of my own incapacity to deliver
such an address as would be appropriate to an occasion of this
kind probably would have deterred me from accepting the
invitation, had it not been that I craved an opportunity to
impress upon young lawyers a few truths which I think are
vital for the ongoing of our profession. You have afforded me
this opportunity, and at the same time, the further occasion to
recognize the great contribution which this law school has
made—and is making—to the City of Houston and South
Texas. Your graduates are found in worthy places on the bench
and at the bar, as well as having distinguished themselves in
the field of commerce, industry and politics. It is my privilege
as a representative of the legal profession of this city to
congratulate you and commend you and the faculty for the
splendid work which you have done.

As this class is about to take its place in the ranks of the noblest of professions, as they are about to undergo experiences involving hardships, disappointments and discouragements, with the attendant temptations to do those things which do not tend to advance the ideals and influence of the profession, it is not inappropriate to speak to you of some of the principles which should govern our professional conduct. It seems to me that there is a tendency to make the law a commercialized business. For that reason, I have chosen to speak primarily on the lawyer in connection with his responsibilities to the public.

We like to think of a lawyer as an officer, because the term carries with it not only the conception of duties and obligations of a public nature, but a degree of independent judgment and action as well. These two concepts go to the foundation stone of professional activities. The present low estimate in which we are generally held, in a great measure, may be traced to an abandonment of central truths.

The lawyer is trained in the science of government. He not only deals with his client in his relationship to private citizens, but a very large part of his activities has to do with his client's relationship to the government, and he of necessity must know the government and its various units, as well as the fundamental principles on which it is or ought to be maintained. Usually, he has been educated at more than ordinary public expense. He enjoys inestimable privileges by virtue of his license to practice law. He uses the courthouse, the public records, the services of the public officials, its juries and the machinery of its appellate courts, its boards, bureaus and commissions far more than any other class of citizens. By reason of his training and his facility for solving and adjusting governmental problems, he is usually deferred to and accorded a somewhat preferred and respectful hearing before all administrative boards which are not strictly judicial in character and to which every citizen is privileged to participate on an equal footing.

Can it be said that a lawyer who occupies such a place, enjoys such privileges, owes no duty to the public in addition to and apart from that of the average citizen? I would not bring an indictment against the legal profession, even if it were appropriate for me to do so. It offers the greatest opportunity for service of any profession in the world. Lawyers of Houston—as a whole—surpass that of any other city in ability and professional integrity. But there can be no gainsaying the fact that we, particularly in the cities, have sunken in public regard to the extent that we exert less influence than at any time since long before the establishment of the republic. We need not look far for the cause.

Crooked lawyers, shyster lawyers, and ambulance-chasing lawyers have not lowered the prestige of the profession, as some would have you believe. There are few, if any lawyers of these types in the City of Houston, and I believe their number in other great cities of the country have been very greatly exaggerated. The sins of omission on the part of the profession far outweigh those of improper and unprofessional conduct. A prescriptive right is lost by non-use and abandonment. While lawyers once occupied a high position of leadership in the affairs of the State and Nation, it is no exaggeration to say that they have literally abandoned the heritage of influence and leadership which was bequeathed to them by illustrious predecessors from Sam Houston to Charles A. Culbertson.

There has hardly been a time in the history of the nation when we were beset with so many local, state and national problems which baffle all solutions. There is not a lawyer with ten years' experience that does not have a conviction that this country—with a deficit of over $3,000,000,000 accumulating each year—is headed for the precipice, which means destruction of property values and ruin to those who toil.

Yet, through fear of his own or his client's business, or indifference, he chooses not to raise his voice in protest to those who are acting willfully, and as a warning to those who may be acting ignorantly. A lawyer who will not speak on public questions because of hurting his client's business deserves the same respect as a preacher who soft pedals a wrong because it may hurt the collection plate. What outstanding lawyer of Texas or of Houston has spoken out fearlessly and publicly on the pension craze which is sweeping the state and the nation and which has become the plaything of demagogues of high and low estate? They properly ask for bounties for the helpless, the aged and the blind, but not for an ever-increasing number who are now—and have been—on public payrolls. Each year we see new groups added to the already-long list, and they have learned to pool their strength to bring political pressure to bear on the legislature. Governor O'Daniel recently said that most of the legislation which came to his desk, as well as bills introduced, were designed to benefit some special group rather than promote the general welfare. Lawyers are not only failing to condemn these destructive practices, but too many times are actively engaged in promoting them.

There was a time when the state was regarded as the chief protector of its citizens, and we of the South regarded our allegiance as being primarily to the state. That conception of allegiance was changed by the issues of armed conflict, as a result of which there was written into the Constitution of the Republic the Thirteenth, Fourteenth and Fifteenth Amendments to that document, and now allegiance is owned primarily to the National Government because no state can deny or abridge the privileges and immunities of its citizens or deny to any citizen the equal protection of the laws. Few people there are today who regret the determination of the issue thus decided because the same resulted in the development of the richest and most powerful nation on earth today, which we have justifiable pride in calling our own, our native land. But a love that does not call for, or engender a spirit of giving to and sacrificing for, is no love at all.

There is a somewhat substantial basis for the fear that the policies of the federal, state and local government trying to appease the appetite of every group of citizens with grants—public and private—bounties, subsidies, pensions and useless high-salaried officials is calculated to undermine the patriotic devotion which is necessary to sustain any free government. I recently heard a public official testify under oath that whether improvements were absolutely necessary or not, "the federal government was giving away all of this good money, and it was up to us to get ours while the getting was good." You have heard that in every campaign that has been staged for the acceptance of public grants from the government. I do not criticize the statement of that public official because the tragic part of it is that he was saying the same thing that is being said by county officials, city officials and state officials all over the entire nation. When public officials the country over seem to be guided in their action by the pork barrel spirit of gouging the federal government, it is time to consider how far that same spirit may be leavening our whole social structure to the destruction of that spirit of loyalty and sacrificial devotion which we owe to the government which protects us. That the government owes its citizenship the duty of protecting its disabled and unfortunate against the ravages of disease and hunger, the same as protection from the ravages of an invasion no one will deny. But, requiring the coming generations to pay for food and clothing and many other comforts—and even luxuries—for the present generation, is a species of dishonesty on our part which ought to be severely condemned and abandoned. Nobody denies it and yet how few people condemn it.

James Otis, Patrick Henry, Daniel Webster, Abraham Lincoln, Richard Coke and Jim Hogg were lawyers who were not governed by their clients' business when correct principles of freedom needed to be proclaimed and expounded. Who is it that has been the defenders of the liberties of Anglo-Saxon people since the mind of man ran not to the contrary? Who is it that wrung from the hands of English tyrants from James I to George III those great principles of freedom, which we claim by inheritance? Who was it that insisted on the Bill of Rights being written into the federal and state constitutions? Who is it that has aroused the people in every great crisis threatening their national safety? The trial lawyer.

When you have been trained for such a responsibility and enjoy so many privileges, to whom do the people have a right to look for leadership in the most confused and perplexed period of our national existence? We have lost our prestige and leadership in public affairs. Let's be honest about it. We ought to have lost it. I do not have a lot of patience with the lawyer who never expounds the principles of government, but barricades himself behind the mahogany desk in a comfortable office during most of the year, living off of retaining fees, and hides himself away to some Bar Association to bemoan and lament the fact that the lawyers are not loved and honored by the people as they once were.

It is much to be regretted that fewer and fewer of the lawyers devote any of their professional activities to the practice of criminal law. More regrettable still is the disposition on the part of some to discredit the activities of lawyers in the criminal courts and look on such activities as a thing unclean and to be shunned by those cultivating the highest type of professional conduct. There are also those who might condescend to defend men charged with certain character of crimes and yet deny their services to defendants charged with the more odious crimes, such as rape, robbery, bootlegging. While some are so situated that they cannot practice criminal law, and others are excusable for their disinclination, still a lawyer who is too good to practice criminal law is too good to practice civil law. Such a lawyer loses some of the greatest thrills of the legal profession. They deny themselves the privilege of studying human relationships in their most interesting form. Few crimes are ever committed that do not have their origin in circumstances of environment over which the accused has little or no control. To seek out the underlying cause of his misdeeds and ameliorate the punishment that might be meted out—except for a full development of his defenses—creates a broad spirit of tolerance in the lawyer which is absolutely essential to his highest success.

And, here, we might ask again if the lawyer has no duty toward the public to perform. Is it not to the interest of every society to see that its citizens charged with crime are vigorously defended by capable lawyers? The unanswerable voice of history is that the fearless, independent lawyers who practice criminal law and strike at the exercises of tyrannical power, have been and always will be the chief bulwark of liberty in a civilized society. When popular fury rises on the tidal waves of racial and religious intolerance, threatening the destruction of innocent victims by the arbitrary exercise of majority rule, it is invariably some great criminal lawyer who steps into the breach and holds high the torch of liberty under the law.

You crave to be a successful lawyer—or you would not have spent the months and years of arduous study preparing yourself to enter the profession. I know you would much rather have listened to something of more practical value in enabling you to launch yourselves upon such a career. I have dwelt all too long in the things which I have heretofore said, but I had felt that they had been neglected. It has been said that to be a successful lawyer requires common sense, common honesty and uncommon industry. Either of these elements is just as indispensable as the other. First of all, he must have common sense enough to know that his function is to equitably settle a controversy for his client and not to prove some legal theory he has about the law of the case. Legal principles are a guide to the settlement of a controversy, but many have the mistaken idea that the controversy exists for the purpose of establishing legal principles. Get a fair settlement of the controversy in court or out of court.

There are no degrees of honesty in the practice of law as there are none in any walk of life. The degree comes in the matter of opportunity. All the dishonesty and chicanery in the practice of law does not come through assisting debtors to evade their honest debts, bribing witnesses or practicing barratry. It sometimes comes about in the less odious form of aiding promoters to mulch unidentified stockholders of their money earned by the sweat of the brow. It may take the form of devising schemes of aiding taxpayers in evading their fair share of responsibility for the operation of the government. And again, it has taken the form of preparing conveyances and releases of valuable mineral deposits unknown to the unsuspecting land owners. Regardless of the form it may take, it is not that common honesty required to succeed. No person—regardless of training—can be an accomplice to crime and become a successful lawyer. His associates in the profession first find it out, then the judges and officers of the court, and finally the public at large, and from then he is held in universal contempt.

If you are not willing to work, day by day, month by month, and year by year, turn back now before it is too late. If you are not willing to forego all forms of dissipation in order that you may have a strong body and an alert mind, turn back before you end up a broken reed and a disappointing failure to your family and friends. There is no substitute for hard work for the lawyer. There is no way to bypass or evade it if you are to entertain any hope of success. The reason is obvious. You are in continuous combat. No athletic contest is more strenuous. Pitted against you are the strongest, ablest, most courageous and persistent of men. How can you hope to succeed unless you are thorough and painstaking in your work?

When the requirements are so exciting, is the reward worth the price to be paid? Many times, yes. Few successful lawyers—in the evening of life—ever look back with regret and wish they had followed some other profession. You will live comfortably, but hardly become wealthy. But why should you want to be wealthy? You have entered a life dedicated to the service of others and your chief joy must come in the reflection on having honorably assisted in making and preserving the fortune of others. When the world comes to sum up the good and evil you have done, if it may be said that you assisted in quickening the public conscience to the dangers that threaten their liberties, defended the weak against the oppressive exercise of arbitrary governmental or economic power, and that you have prevented people of wealth from being mulched by the threat of the mob or arbitrary governmental exactions, you will have done more than if you had led an army or held high political office.

Let no one think that the day of great opportunities for the lawyer is past. It is not a day of bankruptcies, foreclosures and liquidations as some ignorantly believe. His services are needed most in days of prosperity and a rapidly changing social order. We are in the darkness before dawn. As confused as the situation seems at the moment, the nation has boundless resources at its command, and we believe that the youth of the land has the brains, the courage and patriotism to usher in that day. We do not doubt that you will "do your part."

◆◆◆

This Constitutes the Basis of Some Remarks that I Intend to Make to Some of the Beginning Lawyers, Monday, July 26, 1965 @ 6:30

IF THIS IS in the nature of a new experience to you, I hope you will bear in mind that it is also a new experience for me. It is not a post-graduate law course by any means. I am not going to do a lot of research and try to bring to your attention any new law in the decisions or any novel theories that are presently being applied to old law. If I had the time and inclination to do so, I would not because you have had far better instructors who have spent a lifetime in the business, and such an effort on my part would be a futility.

But I hope you will understand that being a lawyer is a matter of growth. It takes months and years. It becomes a way of life within itself. Every experience you have will make you a different kind of lawyer than you would have been had it not been for that experience. While what you had in school will be of indispensable value, in fact you couldn't do without it, still it is only a help to you in making a well-rounded lawyer. You will have to make a lawyer out of yourself by an accumulation of experiences to trying to solve human problems. Bear in mind that one of the functions of a lawyer is to settle human controversies and not to establish theories of law.

I have had in mind, in agreeing to these conferences, that many of the things which are necessary for you as a young lawyer are those which you do not get out of law school and cannot get in law books. Of course, you will acquire all of this in due time, but that is the hard way and the long way. It occurs to me that I might be able to pass on to you some of those things that I have gotten along the hard way and maybe I could save you some of the time and energy you might otherwise expend. If so, it will not only be a help to you, but the firm will profit as well, and I can assure you that I will experience a lot of satisfaction in passing it on to you.

The first thing I thought should be considered would be a

schedule for these conferences which will fit all of you as nearly as possible. Each one of you are situated a little differently from the others. Some of you have families, some of you are single, some live near the office, and others at a distance. The most desirable thing would be in the mornings—say from 8:30 to 9:00 a.m.—but, of course, all of you could not be here and carry on the sustained and regular attendance, which I think is going to be very highly desirable if we profit much by what we are trying to do. There seems to be a difficulty for any time we might select.

So after consultation with some of you and consideration of my own, we decided to take from 6:30 to 8:00 p.m. on Monday afternoons of each week. I feel sure that will not suit some of you. However, it appears to be the best time we could select with the facts before us when we were talking about it. We will try that out until the third week in September when Ronnie will take up a nightly military course of study in one of the schools here. We will take another look at it at that time and if this time of 6:30 works a particular hardship on some of you, we will be glad to reconsider the whole matter before that time. Another matter to be considered was just who should attend these conferences. It occurred to us that the three beginning lawyers and two first-year lawyers should be expected to attend when it is humanly possible and it would be optional with the other lawyers in the firm and with the hope that a sizable number of them can and will be with us at each session. And, of course, it all depends upon whether—in the light of the experience we have with it—we think it is helpful and worthwhile.

Our objective ought not to need defining. We, of course, want first of all to facilitate your own development into highly efficient and successful lawyers in the shortest time possible. Our second objective is to aid you and benefit the law firm in every way possible, because you, of course, cannot attain the first objective without at the same time necessarily furthering the second objective, which is the interest of the law firm. We want you to acquire a genuine love for the law firm and be dedicated to furthering its interests in every way possible and make the law firm a part of you—and if you will do this, I can assure you that the law firm will necessarily consider you a necessary part of it.

We might consider for a moment what your conception of a lawyer is...what manner of man is a real high-type successful lawyer? In this day of high specialization, we have many types of lawyers, such as criminal lawyers, tax lawyers, oil and gas lawyers, railroad lawyers, labor lawyers, admiralty lawyers, and so on. I am sure you want to be a specialist in some particular field of the law. I am not so sure that is not a necessity in this day and time and that all of the specialization we can provide is well and good, but to me it ought to go deeper than that. A lawyer ought to be a leader in human affairs. He ought to regard himself as a servant of society, capable of making a substantial contribution untangling the troublesome problems of our present day.

In 1939, it was my good fortune to deliver the graduating address to the Houston Law School. In that address, I tried to give to the graduating class my conception of a lawyer. That was 26 years ago. Many things have happened since that time, but in reviewing what I said then in the light of all my subsequent experiences, I find that my convictions about what a lawyer should be have not changed very much. The speech has been put on mat by Fentress' secretary and a copy will be made available to all who want one. Several copies have already been made, but I am not sure that there were enough to go around.

But whatever kind of lawyer you cut out for yourself, there are some things you must do and be, which are common to all types of lawyers. You cannot limit these elements, but we can at least enumerate a few of them for emphasis. M. C. (Jake) Childs—still with the firm of Vinson, Elkins—once said to me: "Jim, you don't have to be smart to be a lawyer. All that it takes is just to be honest and work like hell." Well, what Jake said may not have been the whole truth, but it certainly contained two highly-indispensable elements of being a successful lawyer. No lawyer can ever succeed unless he is thoroughly honest. You may say: "Oh, well, I won't be troubled with anything like that." But it is not so simple as that. It may be easy to leave the other fellow's property alone, but to me it means being intellectually honest in all phases of the practice of law.

To be absolutely honest and frank with your associates in the law firm here—to be honest and frank with your clients and tell them they are wrong or that they have no case, to be honest and frank with your brother lawyers at the Bar and who are on the other side of your case, to be honest and frank with the courts and the juries—is not such an easy matter after all. But let us bear in mind that this element of honesty and sincerity is one necessary to the success of every lawyer.

Jake's other element of hard work is no less indispensable than being honest. Did it ever occur to you that so many of the successes in the law are made by traveling an unbeaten path that hasn't been traveled before? It is usually by applying old principles of law to new situations that have not existed before. Every adjudged case was just a little different from the state of facts with which you are concerned. That is what gives you a chance to win if you have justice on your side and deserve to win. My philosophy has been that no man has ever been so tangled up, either civilly or criminally, that you can't do something for him if you work at the job hard enough.

Now, of course, I shall add several essentials to what Mr. Childs gave in his remark to me. You might be as honest as the Apostle Paul and work as hard as any boilermaker and yet, you could not be a great lawyer. The first element that I will mention, and probably next in importance, is to know and love people. If you don't love people, they certainly will not love you. It is just a law of life. If they don't love you and believe in you, they are not likely to hire you. You will not likely bring any business to the firm, and of course, will not be as valuable as you would otherwise be. You must know a lot of people and know them favorably.

Then you should consider how you can broaden your acquaintance among non-lawyers. There are many ways—and you probably have started some already—such as card parties, athletic clubs and other activities of that nature. One of the best things is church work—if you are so inclined to do that type of work. Every church that I know needs help in various ways. They need help in teaching classes, in serving as officers for the various organizations, etc. It will get you acquainted. Join the P.T.A. in your community. They need you and I have never known of anybody being turned down in that organization. Attach yourself to a political campaign. Join the Chamber of Commerce; join a labor union; join the symphony; join the Masons, the Knights of Columbus, or what have you. You will not have any trouble finding an organization that needs you desperately and will gladly take you in if you are in conformity with their principles and purposes.

Now this will run you ragged and take you away from home nearly every night. It works a hardship on you, as well as your family. Try to arrange it so your family can participate with you as much as possible. But I know of no other way it can be done. It is just a price you are going to have to pay. That is where we get our business, and that is where we get our jurors.

I am sure that he and our associates will pardon me if I refer to our own Joe Reynolds as an example of what I am saying. He did a stint in the Marines and in the Attorney General's office before coming with this law firm. He became active in the Second Baptist Church. He did everything that they asked him to do and soon he was substituting for Judge T. M. Kennedy in teaching the largest Bible class in the City of Houston. He was in the thick of the war in Korea; one dinner club asked him to talk on the horrors and purposes of the war; he did it so effectively that he had more appointments than he could possibly fill; he filled the pulpit in many churches; in politics he became widely known as a conservative; when we tried the Jones case in the Federal Court, it was the toughest kind of case, and we did not know whether we were going to win. He, Bill White and myself participated in the trial. I believe there were three jurors who knew him and knew him quite favorably. While it was a hung jury, there were eleven in our favor and only one against us, and the District Attorney recognized it as such a victory that he dismissed the case without any further proceedings.

Now that was all not easy. He is a brilliant lawyer, of course, but not any more so than you and other members of the staff of this firm. The difference—if there is a difference—is that he was willing to pay the price of meeting people, loving them, and willing to do something for them and his country; and now before he is 45 years of age, he is one of the most widely known and successful lawyers in Texas.

Now, next to having a wide acquaintance among laymen such as I have mentioned, I think the next most important element of your success is a wide and favorable acquaintance with the lawyers of this Bar and in the surrounding area. This, of course, can be one without so much time being taken away from your family and will probably be done during office hours. One of the best sources of getting acquainted with the lawyers is to join the Bar Association, and of course, with you it will be the Junior Bar Association. Be willing to serve in its activities. We have been very proud of the fact that this firm has furnished two members of the Junior Bar Association in the last five years—one is Hal DeMoss and the other is the present president, David Allen. They are both making a tremendous success of the activities of this firm, and this of course, is a great help to them. You will meet them at the docket call. I am not informed as how that particular assignment is handled, but it is usually handled by beginning lawyers. The docket is called every Friday and, of course, there is a large aggregation of lawyers there for that purpose. You will have them answering on the other side of the case which you answer, and that will give you a chance to get acquainted with them. Get the names of everyone you can and make it a point to get acquainted with him. It will probably be very useful as the world goes by.

And do not forget the older lawyers. I can say with a wisdom born of experience that older lawyers have a keen interest in young lawyers. They want to see them succeed. They want to help them in every way they can, and just to be frank about it, they like to be noticed and made to feel like they are not forgotten in the activities of the Bar. Do not hesitate to go and make yourself acquainted with them because every one of them will appreciate your introducing yourself and giving your name and telling him where you are and some of the things you are interested in.

And while we are on this point, I will admonish you to be kindly and sympathetic to the host of young lawyers who are coming to the city and seeking a place to begin their practice. They will all work out their problems and some of them that you meet now and give a kind word to will be your adversaries and possibly your judge in the years to come. One of the greatest satisfactions I have is the acquaintance of young lawyers who came to my office looking for a place to light— and even though I could not give them anything but maybe a friendly suggestion and a few kind words—they are some of the most prominent and successful lawyers in the city. Three of them are district judges, and when I go into their courts I feel assured that I am going to get all that the law allows me and that the court will be ready to exercise its benevolent discretion in my direction.

After your acquaintance with the Bar comes that of knowing the judiciary—that is, the judges from Justices of the Peace to and through the First Court of Civil Appeals. This is a far more difficult thing now than it was a few years ago due to the facts that the judges are being added at every session of the Legislature. If I am not mistaken, there are 20 or more district judges here now. Add to that eight or ten county judges and three or four justices of the peace, and getting acquainted with them is a formidable job. You will just have to do it the best way you can. As I said about the older lawyers, when you are in court, never feel any hesitancy about going up to a district judge and introducing yourself to him and telling him what you are doing. He will appreciate it. Up until I went into the Attorney General's office, I made it my business to carry the incoming lawyers over and introduce them to all the judges that were available, and in that way we got the most of them. I shall be glad to carry any of you over there at any time and go through the same process. I somewhat doubt the advisability of three going together because it seems to me that might give a little too much emphasis and an advertisement of the firm. I have found that district judges are just about as human as jurors, and if they know the lawyer and believe in him they can make it easy and pleasant for him during the trial of the case. This is especially valuable in getting postponements and similar exercises of the discretion of the court.

◆◆◆

Appendix 3

The Broadway Plan

Written by Searcy Bracewell, Jr.

ALTHOUGH J. S. BRACEWELL excelled as a lawyer, perhaps his greatest life achievement was the development of The Broadway Plan—a program for financing the building programs of small churches.

Two factions developed in the Harrisburg Baptist Church. The Bracewell family broke away, along with the group which left the old church. The pastor at that time was named Culpepper. He died and was succeeded by a man named Chestnutt, about whom the controversy arose. At any rate, the "rebel" group decided to leave and to form another church bearing the name of Broadway Baptist Church.

This occurred in the early 1930s, which was in the midst of The Great Depression of that era. The group looked to J. S. Bracewell for leadership—he was an educated, capable person in most all respects—being a lawyer, school teacher, practical and endowed with good, old "horse sense."

High on the agenda of the rebel group—in fact the first priority—was the construction of a building in which to worship and hold services. Rev. G. C. Griffith was pastor of the church at the time. The Broadway Baptist Church needed $10,000 for its first building. Banks and other lending institutions were very reluctant to lend money to a church group in those days for two basic reasons: (1) it was ordinarily *one purpose* property, which would be security for the loan and

(2) it being a church loan, it would be bad public policy to foreclose on a church should such become necessary.

J. S. Bracewell—having been City Attorney in the Town of Harrisburg—was familiar with bonds and municipal borrowing. He felt that the pattern of revenue bonds—such as used by municipal entities—might likewise be a sound program for churches. He studied and did research on the subject and found that a church group had a steady flow of income just as did a municipal body.

In hard times, people still gave to their church. Perhaps they were unable to give as much to the church in depression times, but in times of adversity, more people *went* to church and one tended to offset the other.

If the members of the church *loaned* money themselves, they would be inclined to give more liberally to meeting the church budget. Perhaps they had never before taken much interest in the financial obligations of the church, but having *loaned* money to the church (by way of buying a bond), they realized more than ever before that the church had financial obligations. They certainly knew of one—the bond they held!

So the unique idea of church members *lending* money to the church was appealing, although the members realized that it was *their tithes and offerings* that were providing the wherewithal to pay off the indebtedness! Most of the bonds (notes) were bought by church members—although others in the community participated to some extent.

Bracewell was anxious that the program be simple and sound—a good investment—not something to be viewed as a gimmick. He endeavored to make it uniform in those early Depression days. The sinking fund was included as an item in the church budget, but kept in a separate account at the Bank.

1. He calculated that $2 per $1,000 borrowed would pay off the "loan" over a 13½ year period and pay 5% interest (interest payable semi-annually.)

2. He thus made it obligatory that the church set aside in the budget and into a separate account $2 per $1,000 borrowed from the *first* weekly

revenues for the repayment of the debt and interest. For example, if the church was borrowing $10,000, the church must set aside $20 per week to retire the debt and interest in 13½ years. If, for example, they were needing $30,000 for their building program it would take $60 per week. This was the formula.

3. To make sure that the required amount was put aside each week, the church treasurer executed a surety bond obligating himself or herself to deposit such amount into this special account in the local bank before any other obligations of the church were met. Instead of getting a surety company to sign the bond as guarantor, Bracewell's idea was to get 10 or 12 of the active church members as guarantors. This not only saved a surety fee, but to Bracewell's way of thinking, it was a greater security to have people who held bonds "looking over the treasurer's shoulder" to see that he did what he had agreed to do. After all, it was their money (or, rather, money *they* had given to the church). *An ingenious idea!*

4. Some of the bonds (notes) came due and were payable each six months over the 13½ year period—and the interest on every bond was payable each six months. Where? At the bank from the special account which the church had set up and into which the $2 per $1,000 per week was deposited. The church had authorized the bank to pay the bond and appropriate interest coupon upon presentation by the holder without further authorization from the church. Thus, the bondholder had no more dealings with the church as far as the bond was concerned. He or she dealt directly with the bank.

Was it a safe investment? Bracewell believed it was and history proved it to be so. His thinking was thus:

1. Why shouldn't the church *borrow* from its own members and friends the money for building or for permanent improvements if the loan was set up on a sound, legal basis. It was a good investment.

2. How much could the church safely borrow, bearing in mind that the money to retire the bonded indebtedness came from the *first* revenues of the church? After much thought and study, Bracewell concluded that if the church didn't obligate itself beyond 33⅓ percent of its average revenues for debt retirement purposes, it was on safe ground. (This would be true, whatever the source of the loan. This rule of thumb is pretty generally followed by nearly all lending institutions now making church loans.)

3. Would a *revenue* bond be safe in *good* times and *bad*? Yes, because in times of adversity more people turn to God and their support of the church is enhanced—although the size of the offering may be less per capita than in good times.

4. Was there a secondary market for the bond? No, in the strictness of the word. Some of the bonds matured every six months during the 13½ year period. Strictly speaking, you could not "cash" your bond until its due date. But churches being what they are and Christian people being compassionate, this problem works itself out. The church could and probably would call and redeem the bond to persons who are suffering some financial reverses, or at least assist in finding another person to whom the bondholder could sell his or her bond.

5. What satisfaction or benefit would the purchaser of the bond receive?

a. A good investment.

b. The building of the church is made possible— something in which he or she is vitally interested.

c. Most of the local banks had the policy of loaning a member of the church the money to buy a bond. The interest paid on the bank loan usually was almost canceled by the interest accumulating on the bond.

This approach proved to be a Godsend in the 1930s-1960s to small churches desiring to build or expand. Bracewell originally had no idea that it would be anything other than a method by which the small Broadway Baptist Church in Houston could raise the funds to build its $10,000 building.

This was in 1936. During the next few years, several other churches in the vicinity asked him to attend a meeting of the church leaders to explain the program that Broadway Baptist had used. They liked it and asked Bracewell to prepare a program for them. So, by the time of the outbreak of World War II, several local churches had used the Plan.

Building came to a screeching halt during the war years. All materials were frozen and dedicated to the war effort. This included materials for church building. Very few churches were built during the years of World War II.

However, after the war the situation rapidly changed. Bracewell began to get many inquiries about the program, which had been used by The Broadway Baptist Church in Houston. It was then that he thought it helpful to give it a name—and what more appropriate name was there than the "Broadway Plan"?

After World War II ended, the soldiers returned; many people had shifted locations; there was a building boom, etc.; banks were still reluctant to make church loans; hence, all who knew about The Broadway Plan (mostly in and around Houston) made inquiry to Bracewell, who was busily practicing law.

The word spread from Houston, and it wasn't long before inquiries came in from virtually every part of the country. Bracewell prepared a brochure to answer the many inquiries and later went even further by preparing an audiotape explaining the program to the inquiring churches. Wherever he could, Bracewell would go to the church, and his devoted wife would go with him. But the task was too great for Bracewell to go and answer each inquiry with a personal visit to the church, although his two sons and other law partner, Bert H. Tunks, went when they could to make the necessary arrangements with the church. At its peak, we were averaging 30 church bond programs a month.

All was not rosy, however, from a legal standpoint. In most states, there was no legal problem; however, in some states—particularly California—the securities commissioner had some technical objections. Bracewell spent much of his time working out problems—mostly small legal problems—and worked them out in every state except California, where another company called "The Broadway Plan of California" had to be organized and operated by citizens of that state in order to comply with the regulations.

In 1966, The Broadway Plan ceased operation in California and was succeeded by The California Plan of Church Finance. Dr. S. G. Posey was Executive Director of The Southern Baptist Convention of California. Edna Bowling was assigned the duty of operating The Broadway Plan programs for all of the California churches which had used The Broadway Plan.

Bracewell's law practice virtually vanished as he devoted more and more time to The Broadway Plan. Additional employees were necessary; larger and separate office space was needed; stationery printed, etc., and almost overnight, it became a rather "large" business. At first, its operation was merely a sideline to the law office of Bracewell & Tunks. In 1950, it became a business of its own!

All of the partners of the law firm of Bracewell & Tunks (later, Bracewell & Patterson, L.L.P.) helped on occasion with The Broadway Plan—especially the Bracewell boys and their children, particularly Lyn—Fentress' daughter, and Joe—Searcy's son. Lyn Bracewell, Fentress' daughter, ran the business for two years after the death of her grandfather. Joe Bracewell, upon his return from college, also took an active part.

A person who meant *much* to The Broadway Plan was Dr. Noel M. Taylor. He had been Secretary of the Illinois Baptist Convention. This leads to another facet of the business.

Several churches in Illinois had used the plan, and Dr. Taylor became familiar with it. Since Illinois was a fast-growing "field" for Southern Baptist, there was great need for church building in that state. Dr. Taylor and Bracewell discussed the possibility of having the bonds in Illinois guaranteed by the state convention, which would add security to them. This plan was adopted and a surge of Broadway Plan programs developed among Baptist churches in Illinois.

During the late 1960s, Dr. Taylor expressed an interest in becoming associated with the organization. He was offered the position of Vice President, which he accepted. Dr. Taylor was received in Houston with "open arms." He later became President of The Broadway Plan. Dr. Taylor was joined by Dr. E. S. Hutcheson, who had recently retired as Assistant to Dr. White, the President of Baylor University.

J. S. Bracewell died in 1965.

Dr. Taylor brought a new dimension to The Broadway Plan—the *denomination-backed* bond issue which had been successfully used in Illinois. Many other denominational organizations adopted The Broadway Plan as a part of their building program guaranteeing the bonds issued by their churches.

In the latter part of the decade of the 1970s, Dr. Taylor resigned and returned to his original hometown near Carbondale, Illinois. Because banks and other lending institutions began to make building loans to churches and a few issues by rival church bond issuing companies failed, the regulatory authorities in some states passed more stringent requirements which, in turn, decreased the business. However, many churches preferred the bond approach over a conventional loan.

With Dr. Taylor leaving, the organization was without a leader. Lyn Bracewell, Fentress' daughter, was persuaded to take the reins of the organization—having been exposed to The Broadway Plan from her childhood days when she and her cousin, Joe Bracewell, would accompany their grandparents on many occasions when they went all over the country explaining The Broadway Plan to churches.

The decision was reached by the Bracewell family that it should be turned over to the Home Mission Board of the Southern Baptist Convention, since most of the churches served had been Baptist, and the Home Mission Board expressed an interest in having it as part of their church loan department. Mrs. Stella D. Graves and Ms. Betty Hanus continued for several years thereafter "winding matters down."

Several people contributed to The Broadway Plan. Among them were W. A. "Doc" Ruhmann, David Boston, Mrs. Huis Egge and her sister, Mrs. Marcy D. Jackson, Charlene Gilbert, Mary Parker, Barbara Brasseaux, Marshall Stovall, Carl Ableson, Jan Parker, Stella D. Graves, Ms. Betty Hanus, and others.

During the 40 or more years when the Broadway Plan was operating, some 3,802 churches in 47 states used the Plan. Many churches used the Plan on multiple occasions. Altogether there were 5,237 issues of Broadway Plan bonds and a total of over $200,856,562.